D1413063

DEATH AND THE DEVIL

Adolf Holl

---

translated by

MATTHEW J. O'CONNELL

A CROSSROAD BOOK

THE SEABURY PRESS • NEW YORK

The Seabury Press
815 Second Avenue
New York, N.Y. 10017

Originally published as *Tod und Teufel*

Library of Congress Cataloging in Publication Data
Holl, Adolf.
Death and the Devil

Translation of Tod und Teufel.
"A Crossroad book."
Includes bibliographical references.
1. Death. 2. Devil. I. Title.
BD444.H5913   236'.2   76-13207
ISBN 0-8164-0313-9

Printed in the United States of America

Acknowledgments

Acknowledgment is made to the following for permission to include copyrighted material:

Aldine Publishing Company, for B. G. Glaser and A. L. Strauss, *Awareness of Dying.* Copyright © 1965 by Barney G. Glaser and Anselm L. Strauss.

Harcourt Brace Jovanovich, Inc., and Régine Pernoud, for Régine Pernoud, *The Retrial of Joan of Arc: The Evidence at the Trial for Her Rehabilitation, 1450–1456.* © copyright, 1955, by Harcourt, Brace and Company, Inc.

Victor Gollancz Ltd., for Elias Canetti, *Crowds and Power.* © English translation: Victor Gollancz Ltd. 1962.

W. W. Norton & Company, Inc., and The Hogarth Press Ltd., for Sigmund Freud, *Civilization and Its Discontents.* Translated and Edited by James Strachey. © 1961 by James Strachey. Volume XXI of *The Standard Edition of the Complete Psychological Works of Sigmund Freud*, published by The Hogarth Press Ltd.

W. W. Norton & Company, Inc., and The Hogarth Press Ltd., for Sigmund Freud, *The Future of an Illusion.* Newly Translated from the German and Edited by James Strachey. © 1961 by James Strachey. Volume XXI of *The Standard Edition of the Complete Psychological Works of Sigmund Freud*, published by The Hogarth Press Ltd.

CONTENTS

CONTENTS

1

Presupposition

Back once more to Kirchberg in the Mühlviertel, to the home of Leopold Jungwirth, farrier and blacksmith; back to 1944. I looked in at the bellows in the old workshop (shut down now); across the way was the son's new house with the mechanized shop and the old man sitting in the kitchen. I visited the parish priest who used to lend me books, and went to the parish church in Kirchberg where I had spent a few months learning to serve Mass. Twice a week I had used to walk down through the woods to Neuhaus on the Danube, a good half hour away, to the Father Director who's dead now. For Latin, math, and German I went to the retired high school principal in Neuhaus, brother of the blacksmith up in Kirchberg. Then I was evacuated to Kirchberg because of the bombing, and separated from the rest of my class who were sent elsewhere; my mother used to write to me from Vienna. I stayed in Kirchberg by myself, learned Latin, German, math, Mass-serving—this last subject not in the curriculum. An empty room was set aside for learning to serve Mass; "evacuate" means to "empty"; I was evacuated to the Mühlviertel and while there learned to serve Mass.

It may not be out of place to mention here that the altar boy regularly had to get up early; the early Mass began at six and the server had to be in the sacristy fifteen minutes ahead of time. The server put on his robes and made sure his hair was combed and his fingernails clean. He had to learn the *Confiteor* in Latin by heart, along with the *Suscipiat* and other responses.[1] Some priests prayed quickly, others slowly; some spoke clearly, others mumbled. The server had to ring the bell and carry the heavy Missal and bring the priest the cruets of wine and water at the right time.

Altar boys were expected to receive Communion regularly at the Mass they served. Once they got to be thirteen or fourteen, this caused them many a difficulty because of their awakening appetites and the serious sins these might occasion; but in such cases the altar boy could go to confession.

On winter mornings it was dark when the altar boy got up and went off to the church fasting and still sleepy. Only a few lights were burning in the church on weekdays, and it was cold and dark there during the winter months. The server had few eyes on him during the week, since the Mass was a "silent" Mass, with the celebrant whispering his prayers and the server responding. Out in the church were a few elderly people, mostly women, who sat quietly in their places. When the moment came, the server rang the little bell to announce the Consecration, got up from his place on the steps to the right, went to the center, genuflected, meanwhile carrying the bell very carefully, mounted the steps, knelt behind and to the right of the priest, and took the edge of the priest's chasuble in his left hand. When the priest made his first genuflection, after the Consecration of the bread, the server raised the chasuble a bit and rang the bell. When the priest raised the host, the server rang the bell again. When the priest made his second genuflection, the server rang the bell the third time and again raised the chasuble slightly. Jesus I live for you Jesus I die for you Jesus in life and in death I am yours.

Same procedure after the Consecration of the wine. Jesus be gracious to me Jesus be merciful to me Jesus forgive me my sins. The server got up, carrying the bell very carefully, genuflected below at the center, returned to his place and knelt. In many churches the server had a little cushion to kneel on.

Once more I walked to the church at Breitensee in Vienna XIV: Oeverseestrasse Tautenhayngasse Draskovichgasse Kienmayergasse Sampogasse Kuefsteingasse Laurentiusplatz. Red smock coat, white shirt, red tie. Missal, genuflection before the sacristy crucifix each day at six (Mass often half an hour later), walk home, breakfast, school. Jesus in life and death I am yours, perhaps I may become a priest.

Catholic boys do not do forbidden things with girls; the swelling curves modestly hidden are not for you at the dancing class in the parish hall; no man can serve two masters. *Pollutio nocturna* from time to time: contamination in the night caused by dreams, but not sinful according to the moral theologians. Stern demands are made of a server: nothing unclean may approach the altar. Male seed is unclean; so are women; girls may not serve Mass. Not even nuns are excepted; if need be, they can give the responses but only at a certain distance from the altar, if no boy happens to be present in the convent.

The server is anticipating the hour of his death when he refuses to let his seed flow deliberately or when he feels ashamed of his maleness as he puts on his robe for Mass. A server must reject all manifestations of lust, whether he be child or old man; the life-force is cancelled out and rechanneled, "sublimated," in Freud's language. The server is dead to this world: thou shalt not lust; Jesus I die for you. For, during the consecration Jesus dies once again; they speak here of the unbloody renewal of the sacrifice of the Mass.

The death of Jesus makes serious demands on his faithful followers; their chastity must match that of the crucified Saviour. From the dogmatic viewpoint, holy Mass is a sacrifice, a matter of life and death. I spoke too freely at a picnic with the boys of the parish, got angry, should have had more self-control. In my diary I write my feelings of guilt: a server should be on the steady side, people like him to be serious. It is a great honor when the pastor takes a server boating on the Old Danube—two servers and the parish priest in black bathing tights; I belong to the inner circle. The death of Christ obscurely draws me in the cold silent church; the blood of Christ drips slowly to the ground, "I thirst." Soul of Christ sanctify me. Body of Christ save me. Blood of Christ inebriate me. Perhaps I ought to become a priest.

I bring down my violin from the storeroom and open the case. There's the violin I haven't played in twenty years, the forbidden violin. Forbidden by the Reverend Father Superior of the archiepiscopal seminary. No more permission to go off twice a week for a violin lesson, from Boltzmanngasse to Johannesgasse. I'm faced with an *aut-aut* (the Superior uses the Latin formula): either become a priest or go on taking violin lessons; you must renounce whatever is superfluous. After that I take up my violin from time to time and practice scales or play an étude by Kreutzer or Telemann's Fantasia in B. Now and then I play in a quartet at the seminary: Haydn and Schubert; I can play second violin quite well. This kind of violin playing is allowed in free time, but it becomes more infrequent, since I have no teacher. Only one thing is necessary, Jesus says. Gradually the violin is forgotten, as per instructions. O Jesus I die for you. He who puts his hand to the plow and looks back is not worthy of me. Put behind you the sensuous tones of the violin; for you the black soutane, my kingdom is not of this world. I intend to become a priest.

The carpet under your knees in St. Stephan's Cathedral at ordination to the priesthood. *Cognoscite quod agitis, imitamini quod tractatis.* The bishop sits and reads the ancient formulas from a red book. We had already absorbed the words during our retreat: "Understand what you are doing, imitate the realities you handle." The priest must be mortified, dead to this world, when he takes the host in his hands or, more precisely, between thumbs and forefingers, which are anointed with holy oil so as to be worthy to hold the sacrificed Jesus. But first, a long period of prostration on the carpet during the litany of the saints, face close to the floor, forehead resting on crossed arms, a faint smell of dust. Before the act of ordination proper the candidates must stretch out on the ground as men who are dead, chaste, and obedient. Final thoughts of the dying man there on the carpet during the litany of the saints; fleeting associations held in check by the determination to be recollected for the ineffable act. Then you stand up, still a bit giddy; the prayers are finished; silence falls. You get in line, hands are laid on your head, no thoughts now, the candidates wait with downcast eyes for the act of ordination. I have become a priest.

> *We have seen the subject find its certainty in adhering to a historical force in which the subject recognizes itself because this force is the power of a principle of negativity and self-criticism.*[2] Merleau-Ponty

---

Paris, 1954, the summer after ordination. I still don't know for sure what took me to Paris on my own, as a newly ordained priest. My confessor objected. Nor did he consent to my getting a camera with which I photographed the Pont-Neuf and the baby carriages in the Jardin du Luxembourg. Later I gave the camera away; the confessor thought it unsuitable for a priest to own a camera. Vanity of vanities, and all is vanity.

In Paris I go walking almost every day for four weeks, dressed in black suit and Roman collar. Morning Mass at the convent of the Benedictine nuns at Limon near Paris, then into the city: Notre-Dame, Saint-Germain-des-Prés. Excursion to Chartres. I do not want to approach the cathedral primarily as a tourist or esthete,

and need only go into the sacristy and tell them I want to say Mass. When I say Mass in the lower church at Chartres, I fulfill the intention of the builders; seven hundred years mean nothing here. In the lofty shadowed nave of the cathedral I feel quite at home: *quam dilecta tabernacula tua.*[3]

But Paris lies out yonder and I can't spend the whole day sitting in churches. I go to a quiet restaurant on the Ile-Saint-Louis; a priest may eat in a genteel cafe, if he has enough money. I haven't very much money, but I would like to go to a genteel restaurant in my black suit and Roman collar. The quiet, genteel noon-meal of a newly ordained priest; I behave as I should, but later I have an upset stomach from the genteel fish I was served. I see a clear difference between Notre-Dame and a ride on the metro, my kingdom is not of this world.

The priest must refuse the enticements of the world; his whole attitude to them must be marked by a basic negativity; unchaste glances and thoughts may be seriously sinful. Back to the convent and the priests' dining room in the evening. The sisters treat the priests well, they consider it an honor to have a few priests lodging with them. The priests joke with each other at table; one of them recently let a host slip from his fingers and fall into the chalice with the wine; there's a little burst of laughter at this. The priests here are a jovial bunch; one of them has been working for twenty years on a critical edition of the sermons of a fourth-century Greek Father of the Church. Here I can talk as a professional, since my own dissertation on Aurelius Augustine's *Commentary on the Sermon on the Mount* also falls under patristics (or patrology), that is, the teachings of the Western and Eastern Fathers of the Christian Church from the beginnings to Isidore of Seville (died 636).

The Fathers of the Church and the blue-tinted windows of Chartres are the voice of historical continuity: the old masters are related to you, you must represent what they stood for, the Church stands unchanged through the centuries, on this rock I will build my Church. Gertrud von le Fort (*Veronica's Veil*, for example) and

Reinhold Schneider (his *Philip II*, for example) may be mentioned in this context. Such an outlook is familiar and congenial to me, I am a priest.

"What's the use of strength, what's the use of decency? She came to you so lovable, . . . and you, oh Shame, cry Shame!" [4] Six chaste years in Vienna X, parish of St. John the Evangelist. Early Mass and classes in the school and funerals and first Communions and youth groups and family clubs. Late to bed and up early; under these circumstances even the confessor finds it hard to convince you you must make a daily meditation (half an hour, a quarter of an hour). Four weeks between visits to the confessor and only with difficulty is the flag of the spiritual life kept flying; it's rather a rearguard action on the confessor's part, but he doesn't lose heart, gives in for tactical reasons at times, but can also ring up some victories, with regard to the camera, for example.

The confessor represents a strong negativity; he repeats his "You must remain alone." What comes to you so lovable must be fended off; the priest must assume no obligations toward women. It is recommended that you receive a woman only in the parlor, as the confessor does. The confessor is anxious to see me withdraw more frequently for a day of recollection in a monastery. I make fifteen such days of recollection during these six years; my written reflections are very self-critical, and I can only characterize them as negative in tone; at times, however, a certain melancholy breaks through. A priest passes stern judgment on himself, especially when he makes a retreat every three years according to rule, each retreat lasting at least three full days.

Self-reproaches also mark the notes made during the retreats; negativity and self-criticism are to the fore, and the subject has adhered to a historical force in which he recognizes himself because of the principle of negativity and self-criticism that holds the upper hand therein, as Merleau-Ponty says (apparently following the same line as the confessor). I have become a curate.

No one can jump out of his own skin; objectivity is reached only in the natural sciences. In virtue of a principle of negativity and self-criticism the subject has achieved certitude and continues to be a curate, linked to a historical force (if only one knew what name to give it). The Roman Catholic parish of St. John the Evangelist in Vienna X has accepted you and assigned you a room on the third floor; breakfast, lunch, and dinner on the first floor with the pastor, Ignaz Wiesböck, who died unexpectedly in 1957 after a short illness, at the age of sixty-four. Ponderous, kindly Wiesböck at table in the kitchen; he drinks only wine from Maissau, sent him by his brother. Certainty and security with Wiesböck at table in the kitchen on the first floor of the rectory; only on special occasions is the table laid in the dining room.

The slow, thoughtful, tough-willed man drinks wine from Maissau in Lower Austria; my first chief is a peasant in a black soutane, a hard worker in earlier days, but tired now, often nodding over his wine in the kitchen. But he wants to renovate the church; he has saved for years and said nothing, but now the scaffolding can be erected. We must prevent dilapidation and preserve historical continuity. Old Wiesböck spends a lot of time with the masons and painters and gilders; a historical peasant force asserts itself and restores God's house on Kepler Square in Vienna X; then he can die. It is the same will that was shown 800 years earlier in Paris (Notre-Dame) or in San Juan de Baños (seventh-century Visigothic church, Province of Léon, Spain). All these churches in France, Spain, Italy, Greece, Germany, Holland, Belgium, England—the older they are, the more eloquently they speak to me of a historically continuous force when I enter them. *Passer invenit sibi domum, in domum domini ibimus.*[5] Wiesböck renovates the Christian West in Vienna X.

In the hospital room a fly crawls on dead Wiesböck's nose; he doesn't brush it away, it doesn't bother him. The question arises: Is dead Wiesböck's strong will something outmoded from the viewpoint of world history? Most of the people in Vienna X are hardly aware that he has died. The rectory feels somehow empty; who knows whether anyone can replace Wiesböck, at least for me.

It is not an exaggeration to say that any report about a curate's relations with women rouses a widespread, lively interest, and not only among churchgoers. The curate feels many eyes on him when he is in public; many a glance flicks at him in the street. He must wear a special collar, a white strip of celluloid around his neck, as well as a narrow starched rabat of black material under his jacket, the latter being grey or blue with matching trousers. The shoes must always be black; brown is undesirable. The curate may wear a white shirt with a starched collar, provided he wears the piece of black material on his chest where it shows between the lapels of his jacket. Ties are not suitable for curates. Nor is it looked upon with approval when the curate dances occasionally at the parish dance; so the curate sits quite at home in a group, close to a merry young lady who presses her knee against his.

It is not entirely safe for a curate to study philosophy and, later, sociology, and to get a further doctorate at a secular university. It is acceptable, however, for a curate, on the day he receives his doctorate in philosophy (with a minor in history), to go on an afternoon excursion in the company of a woman and to kiss the lady's neck out there in the fields. It is dangerous for a curate to read detective stories for relaxation while stretched out on his bed (loner Philip Marlowe fights for justice but does not despise a passing kiss or love for a night. The strange woman comes to him uninvited in the evening and stays until morning[6]). It is dangerous for a curate to have an automobile to have a secular doctorate to have a sexual organ. The confessor likes me but possibly has never admitted it to himself; he comes to me after confession and explains the meaning of the embrace he intends to give me; he is speaking of what is called the *amplexus.* The confessor is fighting hard in my behalf, he does not want to lose me to the ladies. A faint dry unpleasant smell comes from the confessor's cassock during the short close embrace; the curate doesn't know what to think.

The curate must deal with school children, old folks, and the few young people who come to the rectory; he meets with some married couples every month. Burials and baptisms bring him in contact with the general population. He cannot long fail to see that his work for this general population is rather inconsequential; the newspapers are far more frequently concerned with sporting and cultural events rather than religious matters. The curate feels himself to be living pretty much on the outskirts of society. Religion is just one subject among others in the school, teachers and pupils alike regard German, mathematics, and English as more important than religion. But on the report card religion still heads the list of subjects studied, what does it profit a man if he gains the whole world but suffers the loss of his soul? The lit, indifferent windows as the curate passes along the streets of his parish in the evening; only ten out of every hundred come to church on Sundays; we're not living in the villages any more.

The curate has adhered to a historical force that intends to let no soul be lost, but the majority of souls are rather indifferent, how shall we sing a song of the Lord in an alien land. By the streams of Babylon we sat and wept, the problem of secularization needs a far more penetrating discussion than it has yet received despite the extensive literature on it. The river's tent is broken.[7] (The curate reads T. S. Eliot now and then; not much comes of it.)

In the professors' common room of the Catholic Theological Faculty of Vienna University Emperor Franz Joseph hangs on the wall; throne and altar. At the beginning of his lecture on the history of religions the curate prays aloud before his audience: *Actiones nostras, quaesumus, domine, aspirando praeveni.*[8] Prehistoric religion, religion among the primitives, the historical religions (of the Near and Middle East, India, China, Japan, America, Europe). At the

Catholic Theological Faculty of Vienna University the curate lectures on the Buddha and Muhammad to Catholic seminarians; to another audience he lectures on Hegel and Rudolf Otto (*The Idea of the Holy*, 1917) and to still another on the religious sociology of Max Weber (died 1920). We have rather neglected Aurelius Augustine (died 430) for some time now; we prefer perhaps to concentrate our scholarly efforts on present-day problems.

"The dead masters lift their hands and call out from the grave," Cardinal Borromeo cries out passionately in Pfitzner's *Palestrina.*[9] "Ah, noble friend! who knows for sure what dead men feel? I am an old man, tired enough to die, at the end of a great time." [10]

The subject has adhered to a historical force in Vienna, once the capital of the Austro-Hungarian Empire. Pfitzner's music is marked by an undertone of resignation. The first performance of his work was at Munich in 1917; Lenin was already in Russia; Otto published *The Idea of the Holy.*

"One may expect the call to a renewal of religion to resound through the world with such power and strength as has not been for centuries." [11] I quote this statement of Max Scheler (died 1928) in my inaugural lecture at the Catholic Theological Faculty of Vienna University in 1963, and I add: "Scheler's hope has been disappointed."

Rome, at St. Peter's, December 7, 1965: "The joys and the hopes, the griefs and the anxieties of the men of this age, especially those who are poor or in any way afflicted, these too are the joys and hopes, the griefs and anxieties of the followers of Christ." [12]

Excitement, we're moving forward, the Council is over, I fly to America at the Cardinal's wish, the Church is moving out into the world. In the United States there are no ancient cathedrals and no old masters. I fly from university to university, to sociologists and psychologists and philosophers, New York Boston Chicago Minneapolis San Francisco Los Angeles Milwaukee New York. In the

United States the Cardinal of Vienna is regarded as a progressive prince of the Church; perhaps some rapprochement between modern science and the Roman Catholic Church is not impossible.

The poor and afflicted of every kind somehow get lost in this type of scientific and ecclesiastical policy. The disciple of Christ must never forget whose side he has chosen; sociology serves the powers and principalities of this world. Oeverseestrasse Tautenhayngasse Draskovichgasse Kienmayergasse Sampogasse Kuefsteingasse Laurentiusplatz. The red smock coat, the Missal, the old ladies.

Back then to Vienna-Ottakring (parish of Our Lady of Sorrows at Neukirchfeld) from New York by way of Paris; back to the old ladies; saying Mass for the poor afflicted old ladies as a curate in Vienna XVI. The poor you will always have with you, *cognoscite quod agitis.*

A year later the Pope prohibits the pill, the Russians invade Czechoslovakia. Mass is said for the poor and afflicted of every kind. Gentle Jesus, what crime have you committed that they have passed such a cruel sentence on you? Once again to Kirchberg in the Mühlviertel; the disciple of Christ has achieved certainty by adhering to a historical force that aids the poor and afflicted of every kind. For their sake he has learned to serve, now he must serve them.

2

The Stuff in My Head

Wilhelm Seibold writes: "I'm an elderly, simple farmer of seventy-one, not a writer and not very good with words. I was raised a Catholic; there were and are priests and religious in my family. But even now I've not come to grips with what I was told in school and in religious instruction fifty or sixty years ago. As I look back on my life, I can say without exaggeration that I've believed much too much. I'm old now and must accept the fact that sometime, perhaps soon, I'll be saying goodbye to this world. What am I going to do with all the stuff that flits around in my head like ghosts? What happens, or doesn't happen, after death?" [1]

The old farmer hasn't much time left to wait for an answer to his question. He won't be happy if I tell him I must put him off for a while because I have more important things to do at the moment, such as eliminating poverty or establishing world peace.

However long it may be put off, the death nature requires lies ahead, and no social emancipation can change this fact. Indeed, once poverty and worry about a livelihood are abolished, the fear of death hits home with special intensity; it is as though the surrounding underbrush of other, everyday reasons for being depressed had been cleared away.[2]

Bloch

The old farmer is perplexed, and he is not alone. He is dissatisfied with the religious instruction he received (and, again, he is not alone). Other authorities have not been able to fill in the gaps in his knowledge, and so he is left to handle his problem by himself. There is no universally binding, evident, and indubitably valid consensus he can fall back on that might give the individual, as it did in earlier times, a confidence in these matters, even if only a confidence based on the certainty that hell will swallow up the wicked.

All there is now is a wide range of ideas, conceptions, and theses put out for sale at reduced prices in the marketplace of world views, religions, and philosophies; none of them carry any guarantee. The individual consumer must make his own choice; everyone is free to strive for happiness in his own fashion, as Adventist, Catholic, or Zen Buddhist. All the choices are purely private, none is universally approved, even though the Pope continues to give his blessing *Urbi et Orbi* on solemn feastdays and have it carried over many (but not all) radio and television channels.

In this situation old Seibold sets out to inspect all the things time has piled up in his house. He discovers, among other things, too many objects of faith; his attic is full of all sorts of superfluous stuff; he has to put it in order now, and what is useless must be discarded.

"The stuff that flits around in my head like ghosts." The comparison with an attic (and with cleaning it up) gives only an imperfect idea of what has to be done. The objects of faith that have to be sorted out exist only in your head, not somewhere outside it, and it's hard to stand off and look at them from the distance. Then, too, they are evidently difficult to lay hold of because they are thoughts that pass through your head, and, apparently, your own thoughts to boot; you are dealing with yourself.

It takes a certain courage to deal with yourself when long cherished thoughts have to be tested again for their usefulness. If this kind of courage were common, there'd be no need of mentioning it specifically. But in fact it appears that there aren't many around like old Seibold and that most mortals are quite unwilling to enter their attics, no matter how much discomfort they feel about what's up there.

Of course, if we don't make the inspection, we risk dying as fools.

RANDOM SAMPLE FROM BOCHUM [3]

Once there ceases to be a common agreement about matters in the next world, people start asking for a show of hands, as in a political election. Answers are translated into percentages; the procedure is called opinion research. (In the American expression "public opinion poll" the element of a show of hands or counting votes is clear.) There are companies set up to handle it; it's all done very scientifically, and the job doesn't come cheap. Opinions are determined by giving questionnaires to a representative sampling of a given population; two thousand such questionnaires will give you the opinions of a whole country.

Even the Churches go in for this sort of thing. A cross section of the believers in question are asked for their views on various topics; they are to vote on God, the Bible, and the next life in a way that can be scientifically evaluated. Finally, a report on the results is drawn up; theologians and churchmen then get together to figure out what it all means. The results, by and large, are not very encouraging: you find you're no longer among the majority when it comes to the next world; something has gone awry since we stopped living in small villages.

In Bochum (German Federal Republic) there are about 100,000 Catholics, of whom a random sample of 300 were asked to fill out a questionnaire. The results are representative of the Catholics in Bochum between the ages of eighteen and seventy. Four propositions concerning the next world were presented; the results of the voting (which we give here in a somewhat simplified form) are not grounds for any great optimism. First proposition: "Everything ends with death": 33 percent yes, 52 percent no, 15 percent undecided. Second proposition: "The world will end on the Last Day, as the Scripture says": 39 percent yes, 39 percent no, 22 percent undecided. Third proposition: "Men will rise body and soul from the dead": 34 percent yes, 43 percent no, 23 percent undecided. Fourth proposition: "The wicked must suffer in hell for their sins": 17 percent yes, 58 percent no, 25 percent undecided.

There is a fifty-fifty chance, then, of survival after death ("survival" being taken in a vague sense): that's what we find inside Catholic heads in a large city of the Ruhr, where there is a great deal of industry to provide a backdrop for theological debates. Exactly a third of those questioned were ready to accept death as the end of everything; despite a Catholic baptismal certificate and the religious instruction they have been through, a sizable minority in Bochum were content with an unqualified statement that death is final. (They continue, nonetheless, to pay their church tax.) End of the world, resurrection of the dead, and pains of hell are no longer supported by the majority; hell comes off the worst, with only 17 yes votes out of every 100.

Bochum is not the world, and we may ask what the situation is in the world at large. However, neither the Vatican nor the World Council of Churches has as yet commissioned any inquiries on an international scale; perhaps they already know where they stand with regard to belief in the hereafter among the approximately one billion Christians around the world. Meanwhile, we do have a series of relevant opinion polls from various countries with a nominally Christian population.[4] These polls warrant a judgment that also applies to the two and half billion non-Christians: Wherever industry, large cities, and compulsory schooling have changed the character of life, traditional belief in the afterlife declines as it has in Bochum. Belief in hells and heavens is vanishing in a process that is indeed very slow but also shows every sign of being irreversible.[5]

There has been a decline in the demand for the views supplied by the various agencies, large and small, that deal in Ultimate Questions. The major Churches, of course, have pretty much of a monopoly in this area, but there are other suppliers in the field: in some places, an atheism that is promoted by the State; in others, astrology and spiritualism. The Churches are still profiting by the indecision of many of their members, who for the most part have serious doubts but so far have nothing better to put in the place of what they doubt, or at least nothing that exerts a widespread attraction. In these post-Christian masses the faithful disciples of the Churches feel themselves more and more of a minority; they react with anger or agitation to the rising flood of doubt, but the water is already lapping at their own feet.

In the light of what has been said it is not likely that Billy Graham can bring back the good old days of traditional belief in the afterlife. The results of the Bochum poll point in a different direction.

Sigmund Freud indicated what this direction was in his *The Future of an Illusion*, written in 1927: "If this view is right, it is to be supposed that a turning-away from religion is bound to occur with the fatal inevitability of a process of growth, and that we find ourselves at this very juncture in the middle of that phase of development."[6] Freud also observes:

> I am reminded of one of my children who was distinguished at an early age by a peculiarly marked matter-of-factness. When the children were being told a fairy story and were listening to it with rapt attention, he would come up and ask: "Is that a true story?" When he was told it was not, he would turn away with a look of disdain. We may expect that people will soon behave in the same way towards the fairy tales of religion.[7]

LONGER LIFE EXPECTANCY

The Bochum phenomenon, insofar as it is typical of our times, represents something new in the history of the human race. Before the triumph of industry there was not a single culture that did not unquestioningly accept belief in survival after death, however varied the forms of such belief might be, from ancestor worship to transmigration of souls. It was only two hundred years ago that there began the development (initially in England and Holland) of what has often since been described as the scientific and technological age, with all its consequences for belief in the afterlife.

The human revolution this development entailed may be seen in the population explosion; the latter can be represented mathematically as the difference between the birth rate and the death rate.

What has happened may be brought out by a comparison between two chess games, one long and the other short. The comparison limps, of course, and chess experts will find it unsatisfactory. Let us suppose that in our two games most of the chessmen are killed (so to speak), so that at the end the board is almost empty. (This need not always be the case in chess games, of course.) What characterizes the short game is that after only a few moves the game is over, the board is (almost) empty, and slain men lie all about. Think of these men as belonging to one and the same generation, and all born in the same year. In our short game the men die rather quickly; after thirty or forty years there are no survivors. That is the way it was with the population in all preindustrial societies.

What characterizes the long game is that it ends for the generation playing it only after seventy or eighty years. In Sweden, they play the long game; in India, the short one.

For many hundreds of thousands of years men, without exception, played the short game. High birth rates were balanced by high death rates, so that the number of people remained fairly constant, somewhat as in a chess game where the number of chessmen does not change.

"God blessed them, saying: 'Be fertile and multiply; fill the earth.' "[8]

It was only recently, however, in eighteenth-century Europe, that people began to meet this requirement, but, once started, they went on at a great rate. The birth rate increasingly outstripped the death rate generation after generation; from the mid-eighteenth century to our own time the game has been played in some European countries with very many more men than in earlier times. It has been a wretched game for most of the countries concerned, but a fine one in countries such as England where industrial growth was rapid. In England the excess of births over deaths was almost nonexistent around 1720; it reached its highest degree in the nineteenth century, then declined again, until in our day it amounts to two or three per thousand.

There are many indications that this basic pattern is repeated whenever a country becomes industrialized. After a great surge during the period of transition the population becomes stable once again, but with a difference: the average life expectancy is now greater. In France, for example, the average life expectancy around 1900 was 47 years; in 1963 it had risen to 70.6. The highest average on record was in Sweden in 1962: 73.3 years. The long game is replacing the short game, with both the birth rate and the death rate being relatively low. In some industrial countries the development we are describing is nearing its end, but the world as a whole is in the midst of the population explosion.

We have, then, a new factor to consider: the chessmen stay on the board longer, life expectancy increases with industrialization, and the game lasts longer. But a longer life expectancy also means that people spend a longer time waiting for death, and this in turn affects the way they think.

In India the average life expectancy in 1960 was only 41.2 years, while the per capita income was about 90 dollars a year. The following rule of thumb seems to apply: When the per capita average income is less than 200 dollars a year, the average life expectancy does not notably exceed 40 years. (This rule of thumb describes the condition in which all of mankind lived before the industrial age.) As soon as economic productivity begins, in the form of an increased income for the average man, the life expectancy also begins to lengthen.

Let us now compare the reactions of a Swede and an Indian to their respective situations.

The Indian grows up in an environment in which men do not commonly live to an advanced age, except in the upper social strata. As a result, from his earliest years he sees death waiting for him; by the time he is thirty most of his life is behind him. The high birth rate and the high death rate (or what we called the short game) are part of his experience, since he has frequent contact with birth and death; new life is continually coming into existence around him, but it is also continually being ended, and he takes both for granted. Dying people lie in great numbers on the streets of the large cities; they are an everyday, familiar sight.

In Sweden, on the contrary, a dying person draws a great deal of attention and stirs up a great deal of activity. The same holds for the birth of a child. For, in Sweden the long game is the rule, and both the birth rate and the death rate are low. Birth and death are infrequent events in the life of the individual; in addition to being infrequent, they are spread out over the course of a long life. (As far back as 1900 the average life expectancy in Sweden was already 55.7 years.) A Swede of our day can count on reaching 75, and most Swedes do in fact reach that age. That is a generalization, of course; the insurance companies are somewhat more particular about their actuarial tables and figure things out more carefully. But in the consciousness of men generally there is no doubt about it: We die older and live longer than in earlier times.

To the Indian death is something familiar and taken for granted; to the Swede it is an event. This does not, of course, explain the Bochum phenomenon. We have simply been establishing a framework within which we can discuss the phenomenon. The framework—a longer life expectancy—is unparalleled in earlier times. It is not yet certain just how we shall collectively react to the new condition. But the stuff in our heads is beginning to stir uneasily.

WHAT HAPPENED?

That is what Marlene Dietrich asks in a twenty-year-old song about the millions of dead soldiers who have vanished like the flowers: "Where have all the flowers gone?"

Meanwhile the flowers have grown again, but the dead do not come back to life, and the song's question about what happened is still unanswered. The question isn't about names and numbers, of course; you can get that kind of information from the history books. The question still unanswered, the question we ask in perplexity and sorrow, is the why and wherefore of what happened to us: "When will they ever learn?" This question about what happened arises because of what is specific to our times and unparalleled by anything in the past; it's no answer, therefore, to say "it's always been that way." No one doubts that our ancestors had material concerns, as we do, and fought wars because of them. That's an old story, but it sheds no light on the specific and unparalleled presupposition of modern war: widespread industrialization.

Production happens here, in this life. It grows and proliferates all the time and with ever-increasing speed, so that we are left with no moment for reflection. Terrible wars have not halted it and, whatever the nature of the various opposing camps, it is rampant in all of them. If there is now one faith, it is faith in production, the modern frenzy of increase; and all the peoples of the

> *world are succumbing to it one after the other.*[9] Canetti

---

To put it in another and more colorless way:

> Economics, not entirely by accident, becomes a subject of serious study at an important turning point in the history of western man. This was when the wealth of national communities began, for the first time, to show a steady and persistent improvement. This change, which in advanced countries like England and Holland came sometime in the eighteenth century, must be accounted one of the momentous events in the history of the world.[10]

Population growth stands in a constant relation to growth in production, if we look at the process of industrialization as a whole. Production, however (at least in capitalist systems, according to one theory), is "always too great, never too small": the market always lags behind production, there are more goods than buyers, and the displays in shop windows are always pushing goods that are really drugs on the market.[11] In this situation, wars (and arms production generally) are a way of getting rid of surpluses. Thus there is a connection between production and war, production and population growth, population growth and war—a curious triangle!

What happened? On August 6, 1945, the first atom bomb was dropped on Hiroshima. (A military chaplain offered a prayer before the start of the mission.) Since then, the great powers have avoided war and contented themselves with beating each other in the arms race; now at last they are trying to limit arms production. Our old fears of a supernatural power that can punish and destroy mankind have now gotten a new focus: the "bomb." The apocalyptic descriptions of the Bible have taken on a new reality for our contemporaries, and elimination of the danger has become the object of diplomatic maneuvering, in which mythological visions play no part. The purpose of the diplomatic conversations is to prevent the collective death of the human race. The "twilight of the gods" is, by comparison, simply an operatic spectacle; reality has outstripped myth.

The origins of this unparalleled situation are obscure, despite all the efforts of the historians. Perhaps we must settle for an ironic answer, such as Robert Musil offers:

> But if one asks oneself why humanity took it into its head to change in this manner, the answer is that all it was doing was what every sensible child does when it has tried to walk too soon: it sat down on the ground, making the contact with a dependable and not really dignified part of the body, in other words, precisely the part on which one does sit. And the remarkable thing is that the earth has shown itself uncommonly susceptible, and since that contact took place has let inventions, conveniences and discoveries be wormed out of it in downright miraculous quantities.[12]

All this is not very comforting to old Seibold. He's on in years now and will soon be saying goodbye to this world.

But when he does, it will be a goodbye to our present world, not to any world of the past. It will not be the world of the bushmen or the ancient Romans, but a hitherto unknown world of longer life expectancy and industrial production (including the production of atomic warheads), of population explosion and the decline of old beliefs.

What happens, or doesn't happen, after death? The question has been around for a long time, but the search for an answer today must be carried on under completely new conditions of life and death. The stuff in our heads has to be examined; the attic must be cleaned out. But the amount of stuff is large, and we'd like to know what norms to follow in discarding things. One suggestion: Why not ask, "How does the stuff in question fit in with the contemporary situation of mortal man?"

A vague suggestion, indeed, and not very helpful, but it has the advantage of forcing the questioner to be reasonably attentive. At least we can avoid looking at everything in the storehouse of human beliefs as though it were all equally valid or invalid (and thus a matter of indifference), or as though it were a collection of exotic butterflies in which the ideas of times and peoples long past are impaled for our amusement. If our contemporary situation is unparalleled, then we need to be very alert. Old Seibold has decided to adopt a critical attitude, and we recommend it to others.

THE COURSE OF EVENTS

The man who is happily in love sees the whole world through rose-tinted glasses. But to someone in the hospital or in a great deal of pain the world wears a sad look. In other words, the condition a person finds himself in has some influence on his basic outlook: a laborer is not exhilarated by his monotonous toil as a creative artist is when everyone is fighting to buy his work. Yet it is the creative people who excogitate world views: philosophers of high repute in the academic world, for example, or prominent men of letters, theatrical producers, pop singers, or parish priests. As seen from the lower levels of society, these people are well-off, for they earn money by broadcasting their varying moods. They comment on the course of events on the world scene, and even their sadness finds a sympathetic hearing. Acknowledgment (actual or desired) by society means a good box seat from which they get a better view of the action on the stage.

Old Seibold (see above) is not a writer and not very good with words. But he lives in the theater of the world and asks his questions, seeks to follow the course of events, listens to the news on the radio, reads the newspapers. On the stage all sorts of things are going on: the stage, in Macbeth's view, is "full of sound and fury," but "signifying nothing." [13]

"A tale told by an idiot": the "course of events" is nonsense pure and simple for Macbeth; history is a story invented by a madman.

Such a desolate summation calls for some reply: Perhaps the story of the idiot on the stage has a hidden meaning? If the elaboration of such a hidden meaning be the essential business of the philosophy of history, then the Italian Giambattista Vico was the first philosopher of history in modern times. He died in 1744; soon afterward came the French Revolution and the Industrial Revolution, supplying plenty of material for the philosophers of history. We won't go into names here, except to mention the most recent in the series (there will be others): Arnold J. Toynbee, who covers the whole of human history in twelve volumes (there is also an abridged version).

Philosophers of history display confidence in history: History isn't purely and simply a madhouse; an overall pattern can be discerned. The drama of world history breaks down into a series of acts (though without intermissions between them): prehistory, antiquity, middle ages, modern times. Within the acts the action develops in a series of steps, as it were, with some dramatic effect or other to mark the beginning of each new scene. First, Neanderthal man strides across the stage; then, there is a whole series of new discoveries: the wheel, agriculture, writing, cities, trade, world religions, emperors, printing, the steam engine, and the atom bomb. The most boring stretch is the first few hundred thousand years, when practically nothing happened; but then the pyramids were built and the great empires established. The chroniclers were busy writing through it all, playing the herald, proclaiming sieges and accessions to thrones, and counting the dead. The action continued, generally moving forward and upward: present-day society is better than earlier societies, and there is an even better society ahead.

But it is also a fact that the path of history passes through the suffering and wretchedness of individual men.[14] Horkheimer

---

It is impossible to avoid seeing the thread of cruelty that runs through the magnificent visions of the philosophers of history. Old Seibold is among those who must be written off as one of the expenses of world history, for the World Spirit has no time for him and his private concerns (such as death). There are times, of course, when a reverential gesture is made in the direction of all the dead individuals and their suffering, in the form, for example, of laying a wreath with speeches based on the philosophy of history: "You did not die in vain!"

It takes a certain fixity of purpose to draw comfort from such considerations, especially when you're soon to be executed. Yet many of our political criminals have been impressive in the way they stuck to such an attitude. But, if we reflect that we are all waiting for execution (in the broad sense of the term), history loses much of its glory and splendor for the individual—especially if he finds himself on the side of the losers, as Macbeth did (though he was a king). His comment on his own death was brief and to the point: "Out, out, brief candle!"[15] Or, as another character in Shakespeare puts it: "The rest is silence."[16] Hamlet, too, dies as a loser; the power passes into another's hands.

It is not only royal princes who die with a bitter taste in their mouths and not much philosophy of history left. If we look more closely, we find that the vast majority of individuals never even appear in the history books; their names are not mentioned, they are without significance. The several hundred or several thousand names we find in the indexes of the history books are few indeed in comparison with the vast numbers of people who are passed over unmentioned. Most of our contemporaries don't even make the newspapers, however fleetingly, much as they might like to. According to a rather terrifying statement of Hegel's, we see the Spirit of History indulging himself in countless directions and thus finding satisfaction and enjoyment; but in this pleasurable activity he is concerned only with himself.[17]

According to this view of things, the individual, who is insignificant and plays no role, can only stand by and reverently watch the World Spirit as he takes his pleasure. Most individuals of a given time are like people who happen to pass by a splendid parade of vehicles and watch it from the sidelines as uninvolved spectators; the important events of the age go on behind the brilliantly lit windows, and in the morning they can read all about it in the newspapers.

A nineteen-year-old Englishman, William Devanney, stabbed another young man to death and was sentenced to life imprisonment. His reaction: "It's too bad they won't hang me. People always remember someone who's been hanged." [18]

There you have a despairing protest against oblivion, and the murderer's philosophy of history makes the professors look ridiculous. It's easy for the professors to talk about the course of events, since they've gotten themselves comfortable seats in the theater of history. There they work away at the official interpretation of events on the stage, and later on the school children learn this interpretation by heart, though in extremely simplified form.

And the children believe in it: they believe in the "course of events" and the onward movement of history. The modern mind is inclined to leave the resolution of difficulties to some future social order (Parsons).[19] The settling of accounts in the beyond, in a life after death, is no longer an object of widespread belief; this traditional motif is incompatible with faith in production and is disappearing.

The modern view does, of course, have one disadvantage: the individual dies before things have run their course. He has to leave the theater before the end of the performance and can't wait for the conclusion. But when the end isn't given and the outcome remains unknown, no definitive judgment can be passed on the whole business. Or, to put it with the unrivaled impersonality peculiar to the sociologist: "The question of the personal compensation of living individuals remains imperfectly solved" (Parsons).[20] The official philosophy of history leaves individuals in the lurch; they must look out for themselves.

The professor turns to his next page; further themes require detailed discussion. The lecture must continue, and the vast amount the professor must get through leaves no time for questions.

IMMENSE CEMETERY

Three stars in the guidebook mean: "Worth a visit." Pompeii in Italy is given three stars and is worth a visit. The guidebook observes: "It is exciting to walk through the ruins of the dead city, for in the deep silence of this immense cemetery you feel the invisible presence of the Romans who lived here almost two thousand years ago."[21]

Pompeii was destroyed in A.D. 79 by an eruption of Vesuvius. A thick layer of solid lava covered the city and so preserved a lot of historical materials in excellent condition. For about seventeen hundred years no one thought of excavating here, since the dead deserved their rest. But then (still according to the guidebook) a seventeenth-century architect named Fontana discovered the city as he was working on the roads in the area. The excavations began in 1748, and today about two-thirds of ancient Pompeii has been uncovered. Slide lectures are given for tourists daily from 9:00 A.M. to 4:00 P.M. in an auditorium built for the purpose (no admission fee; from mid-October to the end of February the place is closed on Sundays and holidays).

Fontana's discovery came at a time when Europe was becoming interested in the dead and the various things they had left behind them. Medieval indifference to old ruins was a thing of the past; the modern age was fascinated by the past and found ruins exciting. The modern science of history was inspired by a very simple question: "What really happened?" In the nineteenth century the effort to answer this question went into high gear, as a boundless curiosity drove serious men to the most inhospitable regions of the world (at home the chimneys were beginning to smoke). One such man was Heinrich Schliemann from Mecklenburg (died 1890). At the age of forty he had already made his fortune as a merchant in Amsterdam and Saint Petersburg, and decided to go traveling. In 1868 he settled in Athens and married a Greek girl; this was part of his program, so to speak, for all his thoughts were focused on ancient Greece. He was a man who combined the mentality of a modern businessman with romantic enthusiasm: the first half of life was for industry and trade, the second for archeology. Schliemann excavated in Greece and found treasures of gold, which he gave to museums.

Everywhere, in every possible corner of the earth, the industrial age spends its time digging up the past; public and private monies are poured into expeditions, museums are built and filled with numerous finds from ancient Egypt and Babylon. For a long time the leader in this enterprise was the then foremost industrial power in the world, and the British Museum was its treasure house.

Why all this zealous effort?

Is mankind trying to catalogue its own past as quickly as it can, before it is itself blown sky-high? Are the living trying to get direction for their lives from the dead, the approximately seventy-five billion who have lived on this earth before us? What collective urge lies behind the unquestioned appeal of the guidebooks to our liking for ruins?

The guidebooks single out with stars anything that is, by consensus and experience, historically important; the people managing tourism have a fine nose for what is historically important, and know what travelers are looking for in the market of historical places. For, the crowds of travelers do not regard things as important or even beautiful merely because they are old. The cellars of museums and the scholarly journals are filled with reports on the unimportant. Almost ninety percent of the cuneiform texts from ancient Mesopotamia, for example, deal with financial matters: accounts, bills of lading, inventories.

Old Seibold must soon say goodbye to this world, and the old houses in Pompeii, despite their three stars, are of no use to him. Sunken ships do not rouse his curiosity at all, and he can't make much of gods, graves, and scholars.

We ought to be able to decide in the light of ultimate questions just what is important to us in the storehouse of the past. In this matter we need a norm we can apply in a fairly inflexible way.

> *Purely contemplative knowledge has necessarily to do with what is complete and therefore past; it cannot handle the present and is blind to the future.*[22] Bloch

---

Don't let yourself be bewitched by the old city walls of Aigues-Mortes (Provence), with their medieval look, as they lie utterly silent in the morning sun, in July 1969. This is the "city of dead waters" (that is what the name means), for, though in early times there was a harbor of some importance here, the sea has long since withdrawn, and the people live chiefly by tourism. In July 1969 I took a walk around the walls, which are still intact; the morning was still and I was all alone, a vacationer drawn to the place. The walls, for some reason or other, have survived for centuries, but whether they have anything to say to me is another question. Purely contemplative knowledge can't handle dead waters and dead walls; the news from the past is in code, and if you don't have the key, you're left with just a vague feeling: not enough to make you alive, but enough to tell you you're not dead. The code of the old walls has to be broken; otherwise your meditation is fruitless, and you're left with a charm you can't put your finger on.

The walls of Aigues-Mortes have nothing to say to me, since I can't find the key to the code. The past embodied here is closed to me; I can discern no continuity. The place is really dead water for me, and I must go elsewhere.

The complex of older buildings at Millstatt (Austria) took about a thousand years to build; the place was a monastic foundation. In the summer of 1971 I stood one evening in the cloister (Romanesque style). The monks are gone; the monastery was secularized two hundred years ago, and only the parish church still functions. The silence of the cloister is eloquent for me, since the dead monks, like me, were clerics. The praying voices of the religious can no longer be heard in the cloister, but I am familiar with the old prayers, since they have not changed much in a thousand years. "O God, come to my assistance. O Lord, make haste to help me!" [23] (Gregorian chant is older even than Millstatt.) I learned to sing in choir, and know how the old monks sang; I've sung the same words and melodies myself and still do from time to time at Mass on important feastdays when a solemn liturgy is celebrated. My friends are with me in the cloister, but they do not hear the dead monks singing; they aren't priests, and the (Catholic) Church doesn't mean much to them. Are the dead monks outdated from the viewpoint of world history? Am I myself outdated, with my links to dead monks and secularized monasteries?

Our days by Lake Millstatt are not unclouded. One friend has had a stomach tumor removed, but the postoperational recovery is not clear sailing: he has pain at night, and this fact lurks in the background of our conversations. We decide that I shall celebrate Mass in the Millstatt parish church. The next morning I stand at a side altar, my two friends silent behind me, looking for something very important. "What we shall later be has not yet come to light." [24]

The dead monks were involved in a still unfinished business. The outward forms of their way of life are outdated from the viewpoint of world history, but the process in which they were engaged, in a way that set a standard for their times, is not yet complete; it is still going on. Interest in dead monks and secularized monasteries is, therefore, not inspired simply by impotent melancholy; in this case, the work the monks were engaged in must be clearly seen as work that has to continue. The past is heavy with a future that has not yet come to pass; the key to the code of the old walls is hope, and it is not a buried hope. The immense cemetery of the past holds more than buried hopes and business accounts on cuneiform tablets. Traces of unconquerable spirit are also to be seen there, like unfulfilled commissions left to the living. A walk through the cellars of mankind's memory can be taken with confidence. On our walk we have a comforting light that shines eternally over us: "And let perpetual light shine upon them." [25] The sentiment pervades the music of Mozart's Requiem, where it is not meant as an illusion or an opium of the people. Here we have the musical accompaniment for our book.

RAISED A CATHOLIC

In the letter we quoted at the beginning of this chapter Wilhelm Seibold mentions his Catholic upbringing, a pious family, and religious instruction (in Bavaria). He still hasn't come to grips with all he was told as a child, and the question mark that accompanies the "stuff in his head" has to do with all sorts of things Catholic. What is he to do with it all?

Here, of course, we have a presupposition, very much like the one under which this book as a whole is being written. The presupposition must be tested, as a necessary preparation for what is to follow later.

"Thinking and pursuing a totality or universality": such is the literal sense of the "catholic" principle. The principle came into existence during the first five centuries after Christ, in a Mediterranean world that was in the process of becoming Christian, and it was the end result of passionate conflicts between local Church communities and very diverse kinds of sectarian groups. "In historical perspective the whole seems like a plan—which no one had" (Jaspers).[26] Aurelius Augustine (died 430), bishop of Hippo Regius in North Africa, and himself involved in the ongoing struggle against particularist tendencies, appealed for universal unity under the name of "the *Catholica*." Against a separatist group in North Africa he preached: "What is our aim? The broad commandment."[27]

This Father of the Church points away from narrow local interest to the broader horizon of the *Catholica*, as represented by the common will of hundreds of bishops that there should be agreement throughout the Christian empire, with the emperor as acknowledged protector of unity and peace. Peter and Paul, both of whom, according to tradition, were executed at Rome, confer on the bishop of that see the power to act as arbiter between the others: "Rome has spoken; the matter is settled."

In the struggle to establish the new Christian state-wide Church Augustine finally supports the imperial commissioners who must enforce the edict suppressing the opposition party, the Donatists; the bishop accepts forced conversion as the lesser evil. The Church has, at bottom, never abandoned this path. The *Catholica* has been divided ever since its beginnings; there has been a will to unity, but it has had to gain the upper hand through force. Augustine's initial spirit of gentleness was frustrated by the political realities; the appeal to the broad commandment proved ineffective by itself, and there seemed to be no alternative but to use force. Augustine has not been the only one to make this choice.

In the long history of the Churches since Augustine's time it has become clear that the opposition between universal unity (achieved with the help of force) and local autonomy has not been successfully overcome. The old *Catholica* first lost the Christian East, initially to Byzantium and then to Moscow; both East and West have continued to call themselves "catholic," even after the break in relations. Then Islam forced its way as a third power into extensive areas of the empire and beyond it. The opposition between Islam and the two estranged Christendoms has proved irreconcilable. In Innocent III (died 1216) the medieval papacy reached its high point, but three hundred years later its claims had to yield to the emerging nationalisms of the Reformation period. Since that time the Roman Catholic Church has itself become a local phenomenon, steadily losing importance from the defeat of the Armada down to the end of the Habsburg regime. Today its weakness is generally evident; the industrial age has stripped it of its basis in the believing masses.

The decline of this hitherto highly successful and stable incarnation of power (Jaspers and Canetti have given concise and cogent descriptions of the process)[28] makes it possible now to look back and evaluate. The critique can be all the more instructive in that the object of it was such a model of its kind. For, as a matter of simple fact, we will search history in vain for an institution that can compare with the Roman Catholic Church for success in resisting the restless masses that were its members. All other rulers look like sorry bunglers next to the Church when we consider the long-time effectiveness of the Church's spiritual and political methods.

The careful critique of the Church which we are here urging is not motivated by the private troubles of frustrated Catholic laymen and clerics who do not like to see their Church disappearing. It springs rather from concern with the basic problem that faces the human race in a radically new way today, given the monstrous potential for annihilation that is contained in atomic weapons. This power is in the hands of men who are undoubtedly possessed of only very average capabilities. The question therefore arises of the legitimacy of a power that is greater and more radical than any ever known before, and widespread as well. We must concentrate on this question and resist the tug of specialization so typical of life today. Because of the contemporary situation, the answer to that question is closely linked with the answer to the question of death, both collective and individual.

We now have the presupposition and object of this book. Now we ask the reader to follow us on our guided tour through mankind's memory, for, as we go, we will be inspecting the stuff that flits around in our heads like ghosts. A Catholic education is not absolutely necessary to qualify for the tour.

3

Introduction to Burial Customs

In the animal world burial is unknown, unless you regard being eaten as a form of burial. (Many animals do creep away and hide before they die.) It happened, however, a long time ago, that some apelike creatures decided to introduce a new custom and provide a funeral for their dead companions. It is tempting to see here the beginnings of culture and religion. At the same time, however, we cannot avoid feeling a bit embarrassed as we describe this process of hominization. For, there is reason to think that the human animals, now and then at least, ate the flesh of their fellows, especially their brains, before burying them. There can be no doubt that this was an action completely without parallel in the world of nature, since our near relatives in the animal world almost never kill and eat their like. Cannibalism is a human achievement.

To get information across to the interested reader in a more attractive way we shall mention relevant reports of various archeological excavations, following for this purpose the presentation of E. O. James in his book on prehistoric religion (only certain passages are of interest to us).[1]

In 1927 Professor Davidson Black announced the discovery of a new genus of Early Man, *Sinanthropus pekinensis*, as the result of diggings near the village of Choukoutien, about thirty-seven miles south of Peking. The remains were probably the debris of cannibal feasts. According to Zeuner's calculations *Sinanthropus* is about 500,000 years old. Since this discovery other skull fragments have been found, along with teeth and pieces of jaw and some long bones. These seem to be the remains of the so-called ape-men of Java, who were precursors of Neanderthal man. The bodies were decapitated after death and then buried until they decomposed; the heads, however, were carefully preserved. Since the skulls show signs of injuries, they may have belonged to sacrificial victims who were killed so that their brains might be removed and eaten in a solemn ritual, the skulls being then preserved.

A further example of this ancient custom was turned up in 1939 in the Grotto Guattari at Monte Circeo, Italy. It was the skull of a Neanderthal man and was found in a little grave chamber, surrounded by a circle of stones. Bones of deer, horses, hyenas, elephants, and lions lay on the ground and were piled up around the walls. The right side of the skull bore the mark of the heavy blow. The foramen magnum was opened after death, probably in order to remove the brain for consumption in a solemn rite. All this occurred about 100,000 years ago.

It is also reported that both in Java and in France the custom long ago was to use skulls as drinking bowls. At Nördlingen (Bavaria) a nest of twenty-seven skulls was found embedded in red ocher; the skulls faced the west. These dated from the Mesolithic Period and, to judge by their condition, must have been removed from the bodies after death with the help of flint knives.

WE MUST HAVE CUSTOMS

So says Clytemnestra in Richard Strauss's *Electra* (text by Hofmannsthal; first production, Dresden, 1909). As far as burial is concerned, Clytemnestra expresses a widely held view, and a highly conservative one at that. For, there can be no doubt about the antiquity of our customs and ways in this matter; even the discoveries to which the most recent dates are assigned are older than the world religions.

Professor James again:[2] the earliest evidence for the burial of whole corpses comes from the Middle Paleolithic Period (100,000–50,000 B.C.). At Le Moustier (France) in 1908 a complete Neanderthal skeleton was discovered, face down, forearms under the head, and head resting on flakes of flint; a hand-ax lay near the left arm. Further finds dating from the same period, still in the cave-rich French Dordogne, yielded other skeletons, many in a crouching position. The bodies were frequently placed on an east-west line; gifts were found with the corpses, and traces of funerary feasts.

In the Upper Paleolithic Period (50,000–10,000 B.C.) the survivors were already placing jewelry in the graves: necklaces of shells and ivory pendants. One striking factor is the preference for burying people in ochreous earth. (This is the period of the well-known cave paintings in Southern France and Northern Spain. The conditions are those of the ice age; *homo sapiens* is on the scene and his brain-volume is like ours. The caves of Altamira in Northern Spain, nineteen miles from Santander, are worth a sidetrip—two stars in the guidebook. No smoking on the tour of the caves. The roofs of the caves are low for the most part; the tourist can, with difficulty, make out the outlines of rough drawings on the stone of the walls: the head of a bull, a bison. He learns that the men of that time did not live in the caves but in huts. The tourist feels moved to a certain reverence, for he is here walking about in one of the oldest places in which human art was practiced. It is recommended that he have lunch in nearby Santillana del Mar, a little more than a mile away.)

More recent is the invention of cremation. Sure evidence of it dates from only around 100 B.C. in Europe. The origin of the so-called Urnfield Culture is disputed; possibly the new custom came from the Southeast: from Thrace and Anatolia. Previously, in Spain, France, Switzerland, England, and Denmark, stately monuments had come into use, with stones of considerable size being used for the purpose. Why, then, did cremation become popular in the Bronze Age? The archeologists cannot say for sure.

Cremation was not practiced among the Semitic peoples; consequently neither did the Christian missionaries accept it. It had indeed been the method used by aristocrats in ancient Rome, and down to the time of Constantine the Great the dead emperor was cremated. But the new faith (along with, perhaps, an inadequate supply of wood in Italy) brought back the old custom of burial in the ground. Charlemagne found it necessary in A.D. 784 to punish cremation with death. Since that time, Christian burial in consecrated ground, usually near a church, has been the generally accepted practice. It was a fearful thing to be buried outside of consecrated ground; this punishment was inflicted only on the worst criminals, such as suicides. But cremation continued to be practiced in distant lands such as India and Central America and among many primitive peoples.

Only in the last few centuries did doctors and freethinkers begin to urge cremation for hygienic and ideological reasons, but the Church put up a bitter fight against the movement. Piety and philosophy, however, are having a rather difficult time of it, given the lack of room in the cemeteries connected with large cities. City planners incline more and more to crematoria as the only feasible solution in the decades ahead. (Reports of discoveries of cemeteries from prehistoric or historic times seem increasingly irrelevant.) The bulldozers will be set to work leveling the old cemeteries. Space is limited and expensive in the cities; urns take up little room, and it's even possible to scatter the ashes of the anonymous dead under the sod of a relatively small park—as is done today in Malmö, Sweden. Jesus Christ would hardly object, since he is reported to have said: "Let the dead bury their dead." [3]

PERMANENT MONUMENT, IMMORTALITY

Never has there been such a gigantic concentration of time and expense on the dead as in ancient Egypt; it began as early as the Old Kingdom (2850–2052 B.C.). The cemetery of Giza, west of Cairo, holds a record among the cemeteries of all time. Within a few hundred years the simple grave on a sandhill with a cross of stone over it gave way to pyramids as much as four hundred and eighty-two feet high. The grave proper still lay under the earth; the stone blocks piled over it (as many as 2,000,000 of them) were a monument to the power the king retained even after death. (The average life expectancy at this time was not much more than fifteen years.) The percentage of the gross national product that went to pay for the king's funeral must have been rather high. The aristocrats, too, gave a lot of attention to their tombs. Most of the people, however, were buried as they had always been: unceremoniously and without monu-mentality.

According to Tonybee, life was easy in the Sahara during the ice age; the fauna of the North African parklands and savannahs was like that on the Zambesi today. But after the end of the ice age (ca. 10,000 B.C.) these regions gradually became desiccated, creating a serious problem for the inhabitants. Some of these peoples took a step requiring a great deal of courage at that period: they migrated from what is now the Libyan Desert to the jungle-swamps of the Nile into which men had never before penetrated. These pioneers changed their life style radically; previously they had been hunters, now they turned to farming. The swamp was gradually replaced by a network of ditches and embankments and fields. (The same thing happened in Mesopotamia.) Even today the fellahin of Egypt till the soil after the manner discovered at that time.[4] In this context historians speak of "high cultures" and the various advances these brought, including the literate priestly classes and the growth of royal power. This last phenomenon was especially clear in Egypt, because there the king was also the god.

Here, for the first time, the will to immortality was manifested in a (literally) power-ful way, supported by many careful measures against decay and corruption. Extensive and time-consuming preparations were made for burial; the foremost of these was embalming. The priests were the experts here; they removed the viscera and preserved them in jars of palm wine so that they might be placed with the mummy later on. The corpse was soaked in a natron solution for seventy days, then packed with aromatic herbs and wrapped in linen bands. Various salves and oils were applied to the various parts of the body, in accordance with a detailed ritual and to the accompaniment of prayers.

Once ready, the mummy was taken by boat to the west shore of the Nile for burial with the other dead. It was carried on a sled from the river bank to the tomb while priests swung censers and professional mourners keened. At the grave itself, the ceremony of opening the mouth took place: a priest touched the dead person's face and mouth with a hatchet and a shears, in order that the dead person might regain his powers of movement and speech in the next world. Then the grave was closed. It was important that even after burial sacrifices be offered to help the dead. The pyramids had mortuary temples attached to them, each with its permanent staff of priests who offered sacrifice daily.

There has never been another temple priesthood so extensive as the Egyptian. (The royal temple at Karnak had about 80,000 employees in the twelfth century B.C.) At daybreak the priest would kiss the ground and say: "When I kiss the earth, may the pharaoh have life, and the lord of both lands be praised." The pharaoh, this lord of both Egypts, was to live forever, resisting death with all his might. Meticulously observed rites linked him with his predecessors and successors, and preserved the king against the changes time brings; the goal was perfect continuity and stability in the monarchy.

The upper echelons of the ruling class were part of this picture; they too had their monuments and were embalmed. The rest of the population (about 95 percent) lacked the means for obtaining a life after death that would be suited to people of their rank. They simply went on modestly following the burial customs of the Stone Age and have left few traces for the modern archeologist to find. But the results of the royal efforts have remained and can be seen on a trip to Egypt or in larger museums, which charge only a nominal fee to get in. In the Louvre, for example, admission is free on Sundays. (Only in the United States is embalming now practiced on a large scale.)

Like the monuments in the Louvre, those of the Medici at Florence are worth a visit (three stars in the guidebook). Palace and church lie close together; the family urge to build erected them both, a job pretty much completed within a hundred years. Brunelleschi and Michelangelo worked on the project, the latter on the two wall-monuments for Lorenzo and Giuliano in the New Sacristy. The chapel of the princes is not so famous, but no matter: "Marble and rare kinds of stone were used for the inside walls, and this resting place of the Grand Dukes of the House of Medici has a gorgeous and dignified look."[5] Respect for the great men of this world is a hard thing to overcome; man has an inexhaustible need to venerate something. Anyone who has made a success of life can afford to buy marble and hire Michelangelo to provide a dignified look.

As the result of economic changes in the Europe of that day, a new and modern-minded class of upwardly mobile bankers was busy all over Europe; among them were the Fuggers, the Centurioni (in Genoa), the Soranzo (in Venice), and the Medici. The joint acceptance or refusal of bills created the framework for an economy based on credit, and the interest rate fell from fourteen percent to eight. The new parvenus were capitalists and, being unburdened by tradition, were able to adapt themselves to the new situation. For the most part, these men had earlier been deputies, men of business, or, in some instances, rich artisans, to whom the development of the credit system, speculation, and the circulation of money opened up a new career.

In Florence, one of the banking centers, the Medici had made their way up the ladder; to the fifteenth-century world they offered the spectacle of a financial power such as had never before existed. The sharp Florentine wits had early learned to distinguish the *populo grasso* [the bourgeoisie] and the *populo minuto* [the common folk], the fat-bellies and the poor devils. The time came when the Medici were ranked among the former; they even produced a pope. All this until the glory passed and Italy lost her leading position in the banking world because a sea route to India was discovered and shipping took to the Atlantic. But for a good two hundred years the Medici played a part in European politics; a Catherine de' Medici became queen of France (the family died out in 1737). In his eulogy of the Medici, Jacob Burckhardt, whose eye was fixed on art, unquestioningly passed over their underhanded ways in the areas of money and politics and, speaking of Lorenzo, strikes this lofty note: "As a statesman, let each man judge him as he pleases; a foreigner will hesitate to pronounce what was due to human guilt and what to circumstances in the fate of Florence."[6] Niccolò Machiavelli (died 1527), himself a Florentine, had a far better nose for the power behind the scenes.

The tombs of the Medici are ethically suspect for their grandiosity; behind the artistically meritorious facade there are rumors of less estimable instincts at work. Dr. Freud's sharp eye can be useful here in reaching a more balanced judgment; all that glitters is not gold. We must inspect the tombs of lords and ladies with the present-day situation in mind. Ever since the pharaohs the mighty have preferred to use stone for their monuments, since it will resist oblivion and stir the gaping masses to astonishment through all time, even when the cocks have long ceased to crow at the waking of Lorenzo the Magnificent and all the other "great men" of this world. But the mighty want to survive at any price, and the priests pray more abundantly for them than for ordinary mortals.

We can observe this distinction between two kinds of immortality—the ordinary kind and the extraordinary—as it finds expression in the funerary monuments of the high and mighty through five thousand years of what men are pleased to call "the history of culture." The standards for overcoming death, as established by such monuments, find a late echo among the peoples of the industrial age: people nowadays, as they grow older, are careful to take out insurance policies that will cover their funeral; while they live, they try to provide for a suitable burial with all appropriate display and a grave site that will be worthy of them. They would really like a monument like those of Cheops and the Medici, but of course their means are too modest for that.

The word from Munich is that all graves have to be reused for newcomers every seven years. And so for lack of room the posthumous fame of the little folk is greatly shortened.

THE DEAD KILL

It is highly likely that the post-Christian populations of the modern industrial societies will have to give up the pomp traditionally associated with the dead and their funeral monuments. Resistance to such a surrender is rather strong, of course, as funeral customs show. The whole business of funerals fascinates people, and the reason for it lies deep in that rather disreputable region of the psyche which ever since Freud has been called "the unconscious."

Dr. Freud observes: "The taboo of the dead . . . originates from the opposition between the conscious grief and the unconscious satisfaction at death." [7]

From this point of view the dead become dangerous enemies of the living, for the dead kill, whereas the skeleton, our modern symbol of death, would lull us into thinking that death itself is simply dead. "The living did not feel themselves safe from the persecutions of the dead until a body of water was put between them. That is why it was preferred to bury them on the other side of a river: the expressions 'here' and 'beyond' originated in this way."[8]

The motive for getting the dead safely ensconced in the beyond is to be found, according to Dr. Freud, in the (well-grounded) supposition that the living have mixed feelings toward the dead: tender but also hostile feelings at the time of loss, sadness but also satisfaction. The hostility and satisfaction are, of course, buried more or less deeply in the unconscious; no one can admit to himself his hostility toward the dead. Consequently, the question of forgiveness never arises; what comes into play is rather a specific psychic mechanism known to psychoanalysts as projection. An interior hostility, of which people are unconscious and of which they want to remain ignorant, is projected into the external world and shifted away from the self to others, namely, the dead. Thus a dead person comes to seem like an enemy, and the survivor must defend himself against his malice and hostility.

The funeral obsequies are a means of protecting the living against the dead—it would be hard to formulate a theory in a more pointed way! All the wrapping up and coffining and burying; the heavy stones on the grave; the sealed urns; the dead laid under the floor of the house (as in ancient Mesopotamia) or inside the precincts of a cemetery; the carefully piled up bones in prehistoric and medieval ossuaries; the provision of food, vessels, jewelry, and (as in Sumerian Ur) the slaying and burial with the dead man of wives, servants, and war-horses, so that he may be more comfortable and live according to his proper status in the other world; the repeated gifts of food brought to the grave; the endless prayers and litanies for the dead—all the funeral customs that are as old as mankind have their origin, according to Dr. Freud, in a very simple and well concealed impulse: fear of the dead. And this fear arises in turn from the unadmitted hostility of the sorrowing survivors to the object of their mourning; it originates in their feeling of triumph, of which they say nothing because they regard it as shameful.

Elias Canetti has expressed a similar idea:

> The moment of *survival* is the moment of power. Horror at the sight of the dead turns into satisfaction that it is someone else who is dead. The dead man lies on the ground while the survivor stands. It is as though there had been a fight and the one had struck down the other. In survival, each man is the enemy of every other, and all grief is insignificant measured against this elemental triumph. . . . All man's designs on immortality contain something of this desire for survival.[9]

The oldest burial finds suggest festive meals held by cannibals. When the process of what is now called hominization first began, men had the idea of eating the brains of their dead fellows; the skull was preserved as a reminder of the increased power it had provided. We have little reason to be satisfied that early burial customs should have been of such a kind. For, it means that a violent act which is alien to the innocent animals is to be regarded as the midwife that brought forth our piety toward the dead.

Dr. Freud speaks even more clearly: "One day the expelled brothers joined forces, slew and ate the father, and thus put an end to the father horde." [10]

"This great event of man's primal history" (Dr. Freud's words)[11] actually took place, in the opinion of the Viennese psychotherapist, at the beginning of our entire cultural development. In other words, we must accept that our culture derives from a horrible crime, parricide, that shocks our every feeling.

"The seemingly monstrous assumption that the tyrannical father was overcome and slain by a combination of the expelled sons," says Dr. Freud again, is "a direct result of the conditions of the Darwinian primal horde." [12] For, in that horde we find

> a violent, jealous father who keeps all the females for himself and drives away the growing sons. . . . Together they [the sons] dared and accomplished what would have remained

> impossible for them singly. Perhaps some advance in culture, like the use of a new weapon, had given them the feeling of superiority. Of course, these cannibalistic savages ate their victim. Now they accomplished their identification with him by devouring him and each acquired a part of his strength. . . . This memorable criminal act with which so many things began, social organization, moral restrictions and religion. . . .[13]

The little book, *Totem and Taboo*, in which Freud proposed this theory in 1913, ends with the sentence: "In the beginning was the deed."[14] No one has yet proposed a more corrosive theory of original sin.

THE EMPTY TOMB

Among all the tombs scattered over the earth one has become the object of Christendom's closest attention: the tomb of Jesus at Jerusalem. In it the dead Savior's body lay for three days, but then an angel came and rolled back the stone, as the guards fell stupefied to the ground. The pious women found no body when they visited the tomb of the crucified Jesus on Easter morning, and angels told them: "He is risen; he is not here."

That is the story we read in the Gospels, and the believer may take courage when he hears the Easter cry of triumph: "Alleluia!" Here is one grave that has had to surrender its prey; the ancient law of death has had one exception, and consequently I too, if I am one with Christ, can live beyond the grave. During the millennium between the migration of the nations into Europe and the discovery of America Christ's victory over the corruption of the grave inspired men to a high degree of collective certainty; armies of knights strove to reach Jerusalem and rescue the sacred tomb from the hands of the infidels.

Emperor Constantine had long since ordered a church to be built over the tomb of Jesus, but three hundred years later the Persians destroyed it. It was rebuilt, destroyed again (this time by Caliph Hakim in 1009), and again rebuilt. The victorious crusaders in 1149 built the Church of the Sepulcher whose basic fabric still exists, though modified by many restorations over the centuries. Christians still journey there on pilgrimage, especially at Eastertime (provided there's no war currently going on in the Holy Land).

In Catholic Vienna the Savior is laid in his tomb every year on Good Friday in accordance with ancient custom; people lead their children by the hand to visit the "sepulcher" in each church, especially in the old churches of the inner city. On a side altar an effigy of the divine corpse lies buried under flowers and lights; the golden monstrance is set above it but covered with a veil, as though even the Blessed Sacrament were waiting for the resurrection.

A childhood memory: my mother takes me on the streetcar (No. 49) to visit the old churches in the city: the Franciscan Church, the Churches of St. Michael and St. Peter, and the Cathedral of St. Stephen. Bright lights and the half gloom and a sense of oppressiveness; the whisper of many slow-moving feet, now and then a murmured word. Lofty dim spaces become alien and change into a crypt; the child is being led into the land of the dead where all is still and shadowy. For a while I move through the underworld, having descended among the dead even while the Spring sun shines brightly. Then my mother leads me back from Hades. Later, the teachers and professors will explain it all to me, and I shall have to read many books; anything worth knowing on the subject is in the books.

The professors devote minute study to the accounts in the four Gospels. They want to know what happened to Jesus' corpse: perhaps it was stolen; perhaps he only seemed to be dead; perhaps they buried him in a mass grave and only later made up a story about the rock tomb belonging to the distinguished councillor. The professors are churchmen themselves and for the most part they attach a great deal of importance to Jesus in their Catholic or Lutheran or Methodist or Anglican fashion. But they must also cultivate an academic doubt about the reliability of the old stories in the four Gospels, for professors are regarded by the public as men of science. They work mostly at the universities and must display a critical attitude. It cannot be claimed that the professors are in agreement about the bones of Jesus and the events at his tomb; many of them think it incompatible with their academic responsibilities simply to believe in a miracle, especially such a miracle as this. (We live, after all, in the scientific, technological age.)

Many professors say that the fact of the empty tomb is not scientifically verifiable. Others are of the opinion that the tomb of Jesus most certainly could not have been empty and that his corpse could have been scientifically studied and experimented with just like any other corpse. Still other professors maintain that, on the contrary, the dead Jesus must in fact have left his tomb, for that is the only plausible explanation for the existence of Christianity, even if this explanation is not subject to scientific study. There are also professors who regard the question of the empty tomb as secondary or even unimportant; the answer to the question has (they say) little to do with Christian belief, and the really important questions are of quite a different nature.

All professors argue scientifically and appeal to the results of scholarly investigation as proof of their views; in their works they quote the works of other professors (critically, of course) and incline to this or that view, while constantly qualifying their remarks with "possibly," "perhaps," "not to be rejected entirely," "in certain circumstances," "should conditions permit," or "not exclusively." Professors get to the bottom of things; professors forget nothing; professors test everything very carefully. The scientific studies professors write are read mainly by other professors. Only quite rarely does a wider public learn something of the professors' views on the empty tomb.

A certain skepticism about the historical value of the four evangelists' stories of the empty tomb has become rather widespread among the professors. They point out that the stories are not factual reports but sermons preached among the first Jewish Christians in Palestine. Most professors have decided that not all the stories of the empty tomb are equally old and that we must distinguish various strata of early Christian tradition: perhaps the angels came into the story only a little later; perhaps the statement about the resurrection in 1 Corinthians is the oldest way of speaking about Jesus' victory; or, in another view, perhaps Mark 16:2, 5, 6, and 8 represent the oldest form. Some questions discussed are whether Jesus' body could have been anointed by the women on the sabbath; whether the "three days" are to be taken literally (probably not); what Paul understood by "resurrection," and what Peter for his part may have thought of it. The influence of contemporary Jewish representations of the next world is not to be overlooked.

The handicap under which the professors work is the fact that archeologists are not wholly certain they have discovered the tomb of Jesus. Perhaps all the Churches and scientific academies should cooperate in the greatest archeological dig of all time and finally achieve the clarity about Jesus' tomb that the scientific, technological age should have. What a sensation for mankind if even the tiniest bones could be found beyond doubt in the tomb of Jesus! The World Council of Churches and the Pope would issue statements; the suicide rate would probably climb temporarily. Some archeologist would go down in the history of science as the discoverer of Jesus' tomb; there might even be an attempt to assassinate him.

Until that happens, we may leave the question of the empty tomb to the professors. Contemporaries are asked to be patient awhile longer—if they are interested in this problem to begin with.

DEALING WITH THE SURVIVORS

When a person dies, the doctor issues a death certificate, or, depending on the circumstances, performs an autopsy. Once he has professionally determined the cause of death, the doctor's work is done, and he need only bid a suitable farewell to the survivors. From this point on, the mortician and the priest are the competent persons, and they carry on a very old professional activity with a long tradition behind it and a lot of inherited experience in dealing with the survivors.

In ancient Egypt the whole business of funerals was left to the priests, as we have already pointed out; nowadays, however, there is a division of labor. The people who wash the bodies, the pallbearers, and the gravediggers (plus the embalmers, in the United States) perform the necessary material tasks. They have no contact, or a superficial contact at most, with the survivors.

The funeral director and the priest (parish priest or Protestant pastor or Orthodox pope, etc.), on the contrary, must find the right words to say, for the survivors rely more or less exclusively on them. The survivors are in an unusual situation, since deaths do not occur with great frequency in the industrialized societies (see the preceding chapter, on the long game). It has therefore proved advisable to speak to the survivors in a soft, soothing tone of voice, to be indulgent toward them, and to follow their wishes as far as possible, while also doing everything possible to avoid a confrontation with them. The survivors are, not infrequently, in an impressionable mood; they are often in an agitated state, afflicted by a kind of sad ill humor. The tone of voice adopted by the funeral director and the priest (parish priest, pastor, pope, etc.) is described by onlookers as unctuous, and frequent dealings with survivors make the unctuousness habitual so that it colors the behavior of these professionals even when there are no survivors present. The funeral director calms the agitated survivors with his unctuous firmness; when it comes to the point, he is not to be moved, customs are inviolable. Only in details can he be conciliatory; he has at his fingertips the various gradations in service and the various classes of funerals, all carefully calculated on a business basis. Thus a business atmosphere is created between funeral director and survivors, and everyone feels at ease on the familiar ground of buying and selling, supply and demand. Funeral directors have no need of metaphysics.

It is at this point that the competence of the priest (parish priest, pastor, pope, etc.) comes into play. He has, in some respects, the most difficult and thankless role of all the functionaries and professionals who deal with the survivors. His task is to moderate their feelings during the wake and funeral by actions and words aimed at reconciling them with the inexorable fact of irreversible death. The priest would be lost if he had to find new actions and words on every occasion. And so he has a traditional fund of actions and words suited to moderate and soften the feelings of the survivors. When he comes on the scene, the sobs usually become more subdued, as experience shows.

As we have already mentioned, we find a skilled corps of priests at work in the so-called high cultures of Egypt, Mesopotamia, India, China, and Central America. The priest (parish priest, pastor, pope, etc.) has behind him, therefore, a historical development at least five thousand years old. Some of the formulas used in funeral prayers are in fact almost that old and show a high degree of permanence. (Religions change but the priests remain.)

We must also bear in mind that behind the priestly classes of the high cultures lie still earlier professional men: the magicians, shamans, and medicine men of the preliterate societies. As a matter of fact, we are dealing here with one of the oldest professions mankind has known. The pattern for the behavior of priest (parish priest, pastor, pope, etc.) to survivors is, in its substance, almost as old as the human race, almost as old as the practice of burial. Despite the historically changing shapes and forms, the pattern continues to be what it has always been.

It can be said, then, that the most important factor in the priest's dealings with the survivors is the ritual: the reliable, solid, tested actions and words to be used during a funeral. This is why the professional men of religion usually rely on a written text for their activities. (Not infrequently they know the text by heart.)

Improvisation is possible but must be kept within safe bounds. Frequent repetition of an improvisation quickly creates a new routine in any case, and simply enriches the fund of actions and words with a new variant. The survivors do not look to the professional man of religion primarily for inspired eloquence or originality or ingenuity. They are satisfied if he performs his task in a worthy fashion.

At times, however, the survivors may indeed ask something more of the priest (parish priest, pastor, pope, etc.). They look to him as a spiritual adviser; they want a personal relationship that goes beyond the impersonal ritual. In this case, they may prefer one professional man of religion to another, depending on how they evaluate him in terms of the desired qualifications. Here we encounter the greatest difficulty the professional man of religion has in dealing with survivors, and only a few are masters of consolation at this level. The professional man can be helped by the knowledge acquired during his training; he can fall back on it in delicate cases of dealing with survivors. The widespread uncertainty survivors experience today as to how they should feel must be handled firmly by the spiritual adviser. In no case may he show any hesitation or doubt or even fail to provide an answer.

The spiritual adviser is in fact helpless in the secrecy of his own heart, behind the official unctuousness. He has a strong sense of inadequacy when the widow sits across from him and weeps. Why couldn't her husband have lived a few years more? Why did he have to die just now? I don't know why her husband had to die just now or what went wrong with him; the conversation takes a medical turn. Neither Jesus nor the Doctors of the Church have anything to say about why the husband or wife or brother or sister or boyfriend or girlfriend had to die just now, in these or those circumstances; with the best will in the world I can't answer the question. No Church Council or Pope has said anything on the subject, and even a letter from the World Council of Churches in Geneva would hardly be helpful.

The survivors keep harping on the subject, looking for some meaning in the death of a child who was so clever and docile and happy. But to answer their question I'd have to have a total knowledge of all events and happenings and their interconnections since the beginning of time; I'd have to know just what was accidental and what the result of necessary causes, both globally and in the smallest detail. I'd have to be God himself to answer such a question; but I'm not God and so the question must go unanswered. I'm tempted to tell the survivors that it was inconsiderate to ask such a question; it's a question people shouldn't ask. But I can't say that to them; it would be irresponsible and hurt them.

Perhaps the survivors do not really expect me to give a suitable answer; perhaps they know in their hearts that I can't provide them with a satisfactory answer. Perhaps our spiritual conversation is a game played according to definite but unspoken rules. Perhaps both of us (spiritual adviser and survivor) begin with the tacit presupposition that there is no exhaustive answer to such a question; yet it might be too cruel to put the presupposition into rude, inconsiderate words. What good would it do?

The widow tells me how she recently had to take down the curtains in her apartment and how worried she was about this somewhat difficult job. When her husband was alive, they had always done it together. She tells me how in doing the job recently she called her dead husband to help her as she took the curtain down, and how helpful it had been to feel the dead man near her as she took the curtains down. That's how she talks to me. Then she invites me to share a meal; she wants to talk some more with her spiritual adviser about her dead husband. Yes, I say, it may well be that she will feel the dead man's presence more strongly on certain occasions, but should she still be weeping so copiously? I add that too much weeping can harm the eyes.

4

Do Not Think He Is Dead

Professor Lévi-Strauss is sad. For forty years he has dedicated himself to the study of the "nature peoples" (also called primitives, or illiterate cultures, or simply savages). His principal work, in four volumes, is now finished; a series of other books has likewise become famous. His specialty is called ethnology or cultural anthropology. Before the Second World War, he spent a number of years among the Indians of Brazil.

Professor Lévi-Strauss is very sad, because the savages are dying out; dams and Coca-Cola are civilizing them, and soon there will be no more savages.

Question: "What, in your view, lies in store for the few remaining primitive societies?"

Answer: "They are all condemned to extinction, and that makes me very sad." [1]

According to Professor Murdock, all the societies known to have existed number about thirty-five hundred.[2] They can be divided into living cultures and dead cultures. Some examples of the latter are the ancient Incas and the Hittites; some examples of the former are the Eskimos and the blacks. Among the blacks in turn there are peoples who live in Africa under rather primitive conditions and can therefore be studied by the anthropologists. Other blacks live in rather primitive conditions in the United States, but are not listed among the nature peoples or savages. They are not regarded as primitives in the scientific sense and consequently are not an object of professional study by ethnologists. (Washington, D.C., political center of the United States, is now about 70 percent black. The blacks live in primitive conditions but are not considered primitives in the scientific sense because they live in Washington, D.C., and must therefore be regarded as civilized. The majority can read, write, and count, and own a radio; some of them own a television set as well. The more fortunate among them are, for example, taxi drivers and thus possess a fairly advanced kind of technical knowledge.)

Science regards as primitive any peoples who do not know how to write and do not have fairly developed techniques for mastering nature. Such peoples are still to be found in Africa, Australia, South America, Greenland, India, and some other regions of the world. It is not difficult to foresee that all of them may expect to become civilized in the same sense as the blacks of Washington or the slum dwellers of Rio de Janeiro. The process can already be seen going on in South Africa, where blacks and other savages are being initiated in increasing numbers into the work-world of industrial society; the police provide indispensable help in this area. Perhaps there are humanitarian associations that will build reservations for at least a few primitive peoples, as has been done for the Indians of the United States, so that the ethnologists may not be thrown out of work entirely.

If this is done, we will rescue from oblivion one of the things taken for granted by savages: the belief in the survival of the dead. The belief is evident in, for example, the pious inscription of a tombstone at Lagune Aby (West Africa): "Here lies the body of Emil Bacua. Let those who love him pray for him. Let those who do not love him mock. But do not think he is dead. You will be sorry if you do."

BUTTER FROM NEW ZEALAND

Sir George Grey became Governor of New Zealand in 1845, and soon ran into difficulties in his official dealings with the chiefs of the savage tribes. He tells us:

> I found that these chiefs, either in their speeches to me, or in their letters, frequently quoted, in explanation of their views and intentions, fragments of ancient poems or proverbs, or made allusions which rested on an ancient system of mythology; and although it was clear that the more important parts of their communications were embodied in these figurative forms, the interpreters were quite at fault, they could then rarely (if ever) translate the forms or explain the allusions.[3]

In 1855 Sir George published a book with the title *Polynesian Mythology and Ancient Traditional History of the New Zealand Race.* He was an honest ethnologist; without any false shame, and acting as a loyal administrator of the colonial age, he let it be clearly known what the purpose of his researches was. The question always before his mind was: How could he make the savages of New Zealand aware of their new responsibilities as subjects of Her Majesty the Queen (Victoria), when it was so difficult to communicate with them?

Sir George thus naively betrayed the real reason for his interest in the old stories of the New Zealand primitives. He was engaged in this scholarly work because he was a governor in the service of Her Royal Majesty. Interests, not ideas, rule the world; the significance of butter from New Zealand for the history of religions should not be forgotten.

At this point in my argument I would like to look ahead and

warn the well-disposed reader. It will become evident that the subject of our discussion is unusually complicated. The complexity is due not simply to the multiform character of the phenomena with which we are dealing (contemporary scholarship is agreed that it *is* complicated on this count), but also and especially because all of us are, very much to our annoyance, personally involved in the matters that concern us here.

Tea, coffee, rubber, cotton, and many other necessities of daily life have long since become indispensable to us, and we owe them to the human beings (to their muscles and their suffering) with whose representations of the next life we are here dealing. In this context we should perhaps point out that without the gold and silver that belonged to the savages and without the slave labor that they supplied we would not be in a position today to be discussing the ideas of the next life which these primitive peoples held. The high level of culture of which we are so proud would be impossible without the triumphs of the industrial age; but these triumphs in turn would have been impossible without the meritorious services of all the conquistadors, slave traders, soldiers, missionaries, and other enterprising people who have scoured the world for the last four hundred years in order to spread the blessings of Christianity. Without them we would still be stagnating in the dismal conditions of the medieval serf, and would have neither the time nor the desire nor the opportunity to be concerned with primitive peoples' ideas of the next life.

Many of us may feel horror and indignation at the infamous actions of a Cortes in Mexico (to take but one better known example from earlier Catholic history), as we study the circumstances under which the industrial nations acquired their wealth. But the same history teaches that only rarely have these feelings of revulsion really kept people from enjoying the gains from the infamous actions. More important than such moral indignation with its basic lack of follow-through is the insight that the very melancholy and perplexity we all cannot help but feel as we reflect on the primitives' ideas of the next life is our punishment, and our disgrace as well.

Over fifty years ago, Max Weber forcefully pointed out that the original devotional impulse behind Christian striving for worldly gain had long since disappeared and that "the care for external goods" which "should only lie on the shoulders of the 'saint like a light cloak, which can be thrown aside at any moment,' " had long since become "an iron cage" which it no longer takes a saint to wear.[4] Capitalism is the iron cage which the religious animal has set up as its dwelling and which now continues to exist after the animal has departed. Our perplexed interest in the primitives' conceptions of the afterlife flows from an unassuaged fear of death, and is the price we pay for what we have done and are still doing to primitive peoples. Our so-called spiritual plight can be looked on as payment due for the comforts we have enjoyed.

We may now continue our journey of discovery into the land of man's ideas and representations concerning death and the afterlife, and pursue the program we outlined earlier. Our next point deals with ethnology. Please pay attention; refreshments will be served later on.

WHY DO YOU COME BACK?

The dead person must be soothed by the lulling cadence of endless litanies at the funeral:

> Why do you come back to us? Why do you not leave us in peace? We are here, we are here when you need us. Leave us alone! You come to devour us! Why? Why? We are your children! Leave us in peace! We are here to serve you. We have not driven you away. We have done you no evil. Why do you come to devour us? Why do you pluck at our flesh? Why do you devour us? Leave us in peace![5]

The dead person sings through the voices of the mourners: "I had my house. I had my farm. Then I had to leave, I had to go. You lied to me! You betrayed me, you betrayed me! I am alone and have no one. I went away alone. Now I come back!"[6]

Thus do the Agni, a West African people (Ivory Coast), lament when someone dies.[7] Funerals are an important custom among the Agni and play a decisive role in their lives. The ceremonies last a week and are really completed only a year later in an extensive rite. The higher the rank and the greater the consequence of the dead man, the more expensive and sumptuous his funeral must be; in fact, the death of a dignitary of average rank can bring his family to the brink of economic ruin. The ritual of drinks alone, which are a large item in the funeral budget, means extensive outlays for palm wine, beer, other wines, and especially gin.

Most visitors at a funeral belong to the clan, and each must contribute to the cost. A treasurer or master of ceremonies announces the sum each person contributes. Approving nods or murmurs show that more has been given than was expected; silence greets the announcement of a carefully calculated amount; when too little has been given, there is a lot of chatter that pays no heed to pious feelings. The criticized guest defends the smallness of the sum he is contributing and speaks of what greedy, envious, and malicious people the dead man and his relatives have always been. At this, those present grow furious, scream at the guest, and accuse him of being stingy. Finally, the guest gives in, pays, and asks forgiveness; he's a member of the family once more. On this occasion, a new order of precedence within the family is established, that will hold until the next funeral.

For a year, then, the family neglects all its more important undertakings; all attention is focused on the family prestige, and there are endless discussions about whether enough has been spent. The more a family spends, the more it is esteemed. At the end everyone is thoroughly drunk. This sort of competition brings many families into financial straits, and there is great anxiety about the next death in the family.

The Agni's chief source of income is their coffee plantations. They have been settled in their present homeland for only the last two hundred and fifty years. Before that, they used to move about, looking for gold, and would settle down wherever they found it. As long as the gold lasted, it was used (in the form of gold dust) to coat the faces and bodies of the dead. Today, paper money has replaced gold.

In every village of the Agni there is a church, and once a year the (Catholic) priest comes and collects the church tax. Almost everyone pays it, even though very few regard Christianity as their sole religion. The traditional gods retain their importance, the most significant of them being Nyame. The ethnologists cannot agree on him; one of them notes a point of information supplied by a native: "Nyame is far above us and too much unlike us; he does not understand us and we do not understand him."

Like all primitive peoples the Agni consider man to be made up of a body and a soul that is invisible, immortal, and indestructible. In addition, the body has an invisible double. After death the immortal soul returns to Nyame and the ancestors, but the double roams about as a restless spirit. This spirit is driven by the same passions as the living experience: he thirsts for gin, food, and love. Since he cannot satisfy these desires, he circles restlessly around the living, dissatisfied and malicious, uncontrolled and filled with desire for revenge. The ghosts or spirits are more powerful than the living. Everything is done, therefore, to make the dead person stay where he has gone. He must be put with his dead ancestors in the cemetery of his native village; surely the ancestors will accept him and show him hospitality, and perhaps he will stay with them. But there's no getting rid of him. The dead man sees through all the sly attempts of the survivors to render him harmless; he comes back, and the more recently buried he is, the more dangerous he is. But there are many, many spirits of the dead: how are people to appease them all? Married women are obliged to lie in their dead husbands' bed and confess publicly whether and with whom they have committed adultery. Even that is of no use; nothing can permanently appease the dead man: "I went away alone. Now I come back!"

In their funeral songs the Agni ask: "Why? Why do you come back?" The most plausible scientific answer comes from the psychoanalysts, this time in the persons of three experts who visited and studied the Agni in 1966.

The psychoanalysts write:

> Death means separation and definitive loss, which is the worst of all disruptions. That description, to some extent, also fits mourning as we know it. But there is this difference: we keep the loved one with us as something introjected until mourning has done its work and the loss has been assimilated; the Agni, however, think of the lost object of love as external to themselves, and therefore they enter into a symbiotic relation with it. We might say that among them the introjected object is projected outside again and externalized. Mourning accomplishes its purpose in us step by step and more or less completely. Retrojection, however, follows the law of all or nothing and illustrates the narcissistic experience of omnipotence and total impotence.[8]

Such an explanation puts the idea of a restless, vengeful afterlife of the spirit into a meaningful psychological framework. We Westerners hold on to the dead person throughout the mourning process, whereas the Agni cast him out into the external world where he creates confusion. Both processes go on inside the head, or, in more elegant language, in consciousness. Psychoanalysis introduces a certain order into the stuff in our heads or the stuff in the Agni's heads, as the case may be. The Agni incline to narcissism, that is, they tend to regress to the infatuation with self that marks early childhood, while we are perhaps a bit more mature in these matters, from the psychological viewpoint. In any case, we are not so afraid of ghosts as the Agni are. We are not savages. We have psychoanalysis; the Agni do not.

Let us listen once more to the psychoanalysts:

> While western civilization irresistibly treads down, or transforms, or destroys, most other cultures, the discomfort our own culture causes us becomes ever harder to bear. People ask whether there may not be, somewhere in the world, better sociopsychological answers than we have found. They are looking for social arrangements that put less pressure on man and are more adapted to his nature than our present ones are. Psychosocial relations seem simpler among the Agni, and society there seems better suited to the individual than it is with us.[9]

The psychoanalysts speak, as does their master, of the discontent in our civilization; they visit the savages to look for better arrangements than we have. They cautiously give it as their opinion that the Agni have come to grips with their social problems more successfully than we have.

The psychoanalysts of our day can no longer put the Agni into developmental schemata such as those the outstanding professors of the last century indulged in, with hunters and food gatherers at the bottom of the ladder and Europeans who have gone to school at the top. (In between, there is an ascending series comprising food planters, cattle raisers, farmers using plows, and the urban and literate cultures of the preindustrial era.) The psychoanalysts know that such schemata reflect only our military and economic superiority; that behind the mask of science is hidden the conqueror's sense of triumph. When the psychoanalysts speak of the spirits of the dead among the Agni, they do so carefully, discreetly, modestly, and without any arrogance. They know that as men of our contemporary Western civilization they have no grounds for arrogance.

From this viewpoint (and it is one we may accept), the dealings of the Agni with their dead can be seen as an intelligible effort to resolve important problems. Perhaps other cultures have made more successful attempts? Let us continue our tour.

UP IN THE TREES

It is not only among the Agni that the dead live on. All savages without exception have this idea, although it takes various forms: ancestor worship, belief in souls and spirits, or the doctrine of the reincarnation of the dead. It is always connected with another world, above or below, out yonder, as a far-off land of the dead, or as a privileged place for ghosts in the nearby forest.

(The researchers have been hard at work, and we know a good deal of the customs and stories of primitive peoples concerning their dead. There are many scientific books to be read on the subject; many authors dearly wish to have their painstaking work given careful attention and not just left to gather dust on the library shelves, and we ought to mention them with praise where possible. Any teacher has a strong desire to introduce some order into all the information supplied; he must be strict, and the children must take their turn saying their pieces so that everyone won't be talking at once. Books, after all, are garrulous and undisciplined; they push in, each wanting to be first. Books chatter away and thrust themselves on our attention; each has something to contribute to the topic, but we will never get to the end if we do not put some order into our tour through the ideas primitive peoples have of the next world.)

Professor Tylor (died 1917) is regarded today as a great ethnologist; in his own day his books were exceptionally influential and valued, and even today he is mentioned with praise. Professor Tylor tried to put some order into the stuff in savages' heads, and so he established a developmental series comparable to the process people like ourselves go through as we move from childhood through maturity to old age. First, in Tylor's view, came a belief in the souls of the dead; this led to a belief in spirits, and this in turn to a belief in gods; these stages are parts of an orderly process. Other professors worked out other series of steps, and there ensued many scholarly debates on the justification of the various series (or developmental patterns) as applied to the thinking of savages.

Alas, we must confess that the chief result of all these efforts has been that the various patterns are inconsistent with one another and that we're no wiser than we were before. Which of all the representations primitive peoples have had of the other world is the oldest is a question ethnology cannot answer with certainty; the desire to know and the impulse to create order are pretty much disappointed in this matter. The safest approach is simply to regard the many primitive cultures as divergent expressions of social behavior, as different from each other as dogs and cats.

At the same time, however, there are specific types of attitude to death among primitives; these can be compared as species of animals can (dogs and cats) and the number of types is not very large. One type is belief in souls and spirits (or animism—old Tylor carried the day here). Each type contains a rich variety of forms, again as do the families of cats and dogs, but the basic type is always recognizable (a cat is always a cat).

So much, then, for the satisfaction of our desire for order.

In 1971 a primitive tribe of about two hundred people, quite remarkable in some respects, was discovered in the primeval forest of Mindanao (Philippine Islands).[10] These primitive people, who call themselves Tasaday, live literally in the Stone Age; for at least seven hundred years they have had no contact with the world around them and do not have either sugar or salt. Agriculture and cattle raising are unknown to them; they spend the nights under overhanging rocks or between great roots. They gather the pith of wild palms, grind it between stones, and cook it in bamboo canes. They catch small fish and crabs by hand; their tools are made of stone and bamboo, and they make fire by rubbing pieces of wood together. They live in monogamous families and they sing.

Efforts are being made to keep the Tasaday from too sudden and violent a contact with the modern world. Ethnologists were the first to be flown into the rain forest by helicopter; later, newspapermen were allowed in. The Tasaday have now acquired bows and arrows, knives and sugar and rice.

A newspaper report has this to say about the meeting of modern age and Stone Age:

> As I listen to the flow of questions, a young Tasaday boy sits down beside me. At first we do not make any meaningless effort to converse. But after a while he takes my arm and lets his fingers slide along it. White skin, golden hair—he has never seen anything so strange. He often smiles at me, bemused and trying to grapple with the fact that the world outside his jungle is full of strange wonders. Jack wants to know how the Tasaday represent life after death to themselves. Manda advises him not to ask this question. Later on, when full confidence has been established, it may be possible to discuss such delicate subjects which are perhaps hedged about with threatening taboos.[11]

It turns out that the Tasaday keep in contact with their dead. In dreams they see their dead relatives living in beautiful houses up in the trees, and they receive advice and direction from them.

Here then, as we search for the lost past, we come on a cheerful variation. Perhaps these simple people of the forest have succeeded in living without the fear of death that is so widespread elsewhere. They would be a rare exception to a very general rule. This fact alone is depressing: Feelings of guilt and fear at the thought of the dead returning, and measures taken against the malicious action of the spirits of the dead—these are what characterize the animistic world. Dr. Freud's intuition (cf. previous chapter) is confirmed by ethnology: the dead kill.

THE FATE OF SOULS

The representations of the soul among primitive people resemble a great tree full of birds whose varied twittering creates a confused mass of sound; how can anyone make head or tail of it? The professors of ethnology try in vain to put order into it. They make up series of types of soul, but can't make things really fit together: organ-souls, ego-souls, free-souls, growth-souls, etc., etc. The lines of demarcation are too fluid; there is no unifying theory.

At least two souls dwell in the breast of most primitives, as they do in the Agni, and death has a different fate in store for each. An orderly, Western-style distinction between body and soul is hardly to the point (primitive though such a distinction is); still less, a distinction between departed souls and souls still embodied on earth. In dreams, myths, and fairy tales, a soul glides from a sleeper's mouth in the form of a mouse (for example), goes about its business, and returns before the sleeper awakes. At times, a departed soul looks for a new dwelling in a newborn child; this is called reincarnation.

Frequently, a soul after death must pass through many dangers on its journey to the next world: it must cross a torrential river, pass over abysses on swaying bridges, negotiate narrow pathways in mountains, undergo trials, conquer demons, and, in general, overcome many kinds of obstacles.

All this may be interpreted as representing the mourning process the survivors must undergo and as expressing the conflict between their contradictory feelings, since, on the one hand, for their sake the dead man must go away, far away if possible, while, on the other, the survivors also want to hold on to him, and they feel the loss of him keenly. The dead man's journey would then be the manifestation of the survivors' desire that he gradually disappear from their lives; the obstacles on the journey would express their desire not to let him go, since the loss is also painful to them and the conflict between grief and satisfaction remains intense.

According as the guilt feelings of the survivors are still strong or have, on the contrary, begun to fade, the lot of the departed souls is conceived by various peoples and tribes to be either wretched or happy; they are in Hades or in Valhalla. (Among warlike primitives the courageous fighter is assured of a pleasant lot.) What is almost completely lacking among primitives, however, is the savage, passionate torment of hell as a possible destiny for the departed and a fearful threat for the living.

Buddhism, Christianity, and Islam, on the other hand, cannot manage without hell (more on this later). But among primitives the idea of punishment in the other world is almost completely missing, as is a belief in a final judgment as the definitive restoration of a justice that has been only imperfectly realized on earth.[12]

Thus, anxiety too has its developmental history and its progress. In comparison with the fantasies about hell that we find in Dante the poet and Bosch the painter (and the ideas such fantasies presuppose in the heads of medieval Christians generally), the fear primitives have of the spirits of the dead seems quite moderate. It was high time for the missionaries to come and tell the primitives about hell.

The reason for the backwardness of primitives as far as the fear of hell is concerned is probably to be found in the backwardness of their economies and work experience, as well as in the lack of any but a rudimentary development of social classes among primitive peoples and tribes. Or, to put it the other way around: Hell is a cultural phenomenon that makes its appearance along with cities, writing, and trade, and therefore comes on the scene in the so-called high cultures of the preindustrial era.

The punishment of hell serves in the literate cultures as an efficacious social tool for channeling the latent aggressions that are present in these developed societies; the study of hell provides us with information on the subterranean mechanics of the soul in these societies. Primitives do not need any of this; they are not sufficiently advanced.

HALF AN HOUR AFTER DEATH

The fifth edition of Dominic M. Prümmer's *Handbook of Moral Theology* appeared in 1941 (in Latin), bearing the imprimatur of the appropriate ecclesiastical authority and printed on India paper. The book is (or was) an internationally used study-aid for Catholic confessors; it painstakingly incorporated the latest decisions of the Roman Curia. Many priests, including the present writer, studied their Prümmer; the book situates us in modern times, Central Europe. We ask pardon for the short interruption in our tour of primitive ideas of the other world; think of it as a digression or excursus.

"Pastors of souls have a grave obligation to administer this sacrament [Last Anointing] to those of their subjects who reasonably [*rationabiliter*] request it."[13] Thus says Prümmer in his clear Latin, and he but repeats what was said in the Code of Canon Law. Because the obligation is such a serious one, Catholic rectories (in Catholic Central Europe) have a bell which people call the "viaticum bell"; day or night the priest must be within reach so that he may provide the dying person with the consolations of holy religion.

The request to the priest that he administer the Last Anointing may sometimes be an unreasonable one. That is, relatives sometimes want to spare the dying person the sight of the priest as long as possible, and so the priest often arrives only after the dying person has already sunk into a deep coma. It may even happen that he comes entirely too late; the relatives have waited too long. Death came sooner than they had expected, and now the priest must hurry with the oils, since only the living, not the dead, may be anointed. Last Anointing is one of the seven sacraments of the Catholic

Church, and these are meant for the living; there are no sacraments for the dead.

At times, then, a distressing case occurs. The priest comes a little too late with the oils, yet the relatives want something effective done. After all, the dead man is still warm! Prümmer's *Handbook* has the solution: "Since it is not certain exactly when the soul actually departs [*egrediatur*] from the body the sacrament may be administered conditionally up to half an hour after apparent death." [14] Thus the priest has half an hour in which to do his job in a case of unexpected death; in these circumstances he takes a small precaution as he administers the anointing, by saying to the dead person: "If you are still alive." For it remains uncertain for at least half an hour whether the soul in fact left its dwelling for good at the moment of seeming death. According to the teaching of the Church, man is composed of body and soul, and death is a separation of the two. The soul leaves (*egrediatur*) and the body stays behind.

We may think that this conception dates from the preindustrial era of human history and corresponds directly to the way primitives think. Thus the priest enters into a very ancient heritage when he carries out his prescribed task; in thought, we are in the company of the primitives.

The primitive mind is, in the fullest meaning of the word, imperishable.[15] Freud

---

The advantage the priest has over his primitive colleagues in Africa or Polynesia is that he can use a watch to determine when a half hour has passed. The medicine men must rely on more primitive means at this point.

BLOOD RELATIONS IN THE OTHER WORLD

Throughout the world, relatives hurry to the scene when a death occurs, and they expect to be given food and drink when the funeral is over. This is true not just of primitives; the familial aspect of death is still discernible in the modern large city too. It is much weaker, of course, since the importance of the clan has recently declined and given way to a concentration on the nuclear family of father, mother, and child. The aristocracy is still interested in matters genealogical; otherwise, hardly anyone remembers what happened before grandfather came on the scene.

A long time ago the Shoshone Indians lived on a high desert plateau in North America.[16] The region was unpromising and the population small. There were no towns or cities; it took a large area to provide a minimum of food for a family which depended on hunting small animals and gathering roots. Several families would cooperate in rabbit hunts; on these occasions marriages were arranged.

Double marriages were preferred, that is, sons and daughters of one family marrying daughters and sons of another; in this way, small groups came into existence that could better defend themselves against enemies. If too many girls were born, they had to be satisfied with sharing a husband; if too many males, they had to share a wife. But monogamy and small families were the rule at that time, and no one needed to keep an eye on the various family trees.

Some Shoshones wandered to an area where small-scale agriculture was possible. There was water, and stone from the mountains for building houses. A degree of division of labor was now required, with the men continuing to hunt and the women doing the farming. The men were usually away; the women—grandmother, mother, daughters—kept house. In this connection anthropologists speak of a matrilocal household. The Shoshones kept this arrangement when for some reason (perhaps pressure from the

Apaches) they moved south into Arizona. In Arizona they were called the Hopi Indians and became the object of extensive ethnological study.

The Hopi, as we said, kept the matrilocal household even in the villages they now lived in on the mesas atop the high flat rock-spurs of Arizona. But now that they lived in closer proximity to one another, a new problem arose. The men who married did not disappear as they had in the thinly settled high plateau, but simply moved around the corner as it were. Moreover, they too had become farmers and worked near the village, so that their long absences were no longer the rule. The threat involved in the close crowding of related families was handled in a way we find practiced by other primitive peoples as well. Descent was matrilinear not only in fact but to some extent officially; here then we have a matrilinear order (vs. patrilinear, i.e., with descent reckoned according to the paternal side; both methods have disappeared among us).

The maternal household retained the greater prestige because names (based on totem animals) were derived from it and because the women had charge of the fetishes. The name and thus the relation to the maternal home and family were kept by daughters who married and moved away. Thus the clan (rabbit, snake, etc.) came into existence as a higher level system of relationships with its special name and as the most important group in the society (we still see remnants of this system in Scotland today).

The story of the Hopi is rather unimportant in itself, but it illustrates a widespread pattern: As soon as the clan comes into existence (as a number of households, all having the same name and scattered over a wide area), there is a felt need of ancestors, that is, of assigning the clan an origin in a common ancestral father (or mother). Then comes ancestor worship as a widespread phenomenon among primitive peoples, especially in Africa and East Asia. The dead ancestors give the related individuals a greater sense of group identity.

When kings enter the picture, the interest in genealogy deepens; prominent ancestors are long remembered, and their descendants even erect statues of them. At set times sacrifices are conscientiously offered to them in places expressly chosen for this purpose. The malice that otherwise characterizes the spirits of the dead is very much moderated in the case of ancestors; they have been dead for a long time, and the mourning process has long since been completed. Show them respect, and they will prove friendly and helpful, promoting the fertility of vegetation, animals, and men, and giving their clan protection from danger as well as prosperity and the prestige that goes with it.

PIETY OF THE CANNIBALS

Melanesia is an area of the Southwest Pacific and includes New Guinea, the Bismarck Archipelago, Santa Cruz, and some other islands. Like the rest of the South Sea, Melanesia was settled from Asia, but earlier than other regions in that part of the world. The oldest culture (only remnants now exist) was that of the Pygmies.

The Melanesians make great display of the skulls of the dead; the tourist is urged not to draw any hasty conclusions. We must distinguish between the lovingly preserved skulls of the ancestors, which are attached to boards on the walls of the meeting houses, and the heads of slain enemies that have been taken as trophies. In earlier times, a skull thus won in battle was an indispensable proof that a man was ready for marriage; every additional skull notably increased his potency.

There is a word in the Melanesian language that has especially fascinated ethnologists and scholars in the science of religions: the word *mana. Mana* is taken to mean a power that is to be found in every living thing and can be transferred to inanimate objects as well. The skull taken in battle has *mana;* the skulls of the ancestors have *mana;* and the eating of human flesh brings an increase in *mana.* Cannibalism is a ritual phenomenon and is not to be explained as resulting from a lack of food. We are dealing here with a pious custom. (The great antiquity of the custom was brought out in the previous chapter.)

Old Seibold (see chapter 2) is growing impatient. What does, or doesn't, come after death? He can't make much of cannibalism! We'll have to sketch a provisional summary, so that he won't lose heart and stop reading. Children and fools tell the truth, says a proverb. Well, children and fools and primitives have been scientifically linked for some time now (Dr. Freud made the connection in an exemplary way.) The study of prehistory (in the form of archeology) and the study of primitive peoples (in the form of ethnology) should tell us something about our own childish, primitive, foolish nature; perhaps we'll be the wiser for it. Excavated tombs, burial customs, and stories of the other world help industrial man to know his own past; in studying them he is leafing through the family album.

Meanwhile, industrial civilization is becoming ever more widespread and soon will be the only one left on earth. Social change is swallowing up the primitives along with their chiefs and their ideas of the other world, and even the somewhat more advanced medieval sheikhs have but a short time left. Standard Oil and U.S. Steel are already at work.

If the modern automobile driver (as a consumer of oil and steel) wants a bit of metaphysics, where is he to get it? The driver is not a cannibal and can't eat his metaphysics the way the Melanesians did who believed that *mana* resided in the slain enemy. The relationship to the transcendent has become more complicated for the driver. In times of quiet reflection the driver feels sad at all that he has lost. By rights he should have lived on a South Sea island, as Gauguin the painter did; the world was still an orderly place there. Alas, these moments of thoughtfulness are only moments of wishful thinking and leave no trace; the automobile is more important.

Can the modern driver keep both his car and primitive man's belief in the other world? One thing is sure: belief in life after death is older even than the great religions; it arose at a very early stage of culture; its origins are questionable and thoroughly ambiguous, if not downright suspect. Another story that primitives tell is that man began as good but then through some mishap became evil; the story is, however, not well authenticated. Whether the primitives with their belief in the other world are a good thing or a bad is a useless question that gets us no farther; it can be answered in different ways, depending on your viewpoint. The modern viewpoint is clear enough: the driver drives his vehicle at the expense of the primitives, and the latter must now disappear to make way for progress. The interest in primitive thinking is really an idle one, since, in fact, we are steadily eliminating primitive thinking, including their ideas of the other world (cf. the Bochum poll).

At the same time, there is something that argues for the survival of primitive ideas of the other world even among drivers, and it has the support of the Churches. I am referring to Dr. Freud's discovery: "The primitive mind is, in the fullest meaning of the word, imperishable."

Dr. Freud considers belief in another world to be an illusion (not an error):

> What is characteristic of illusions is that they are derived from human wishes. In this respect they come near to psychiatric delusions. But they differ from them, too, apart from the more complicated structure of delusions. In the case of delusions, we emphasize as essential their being in contradiction to reality. Illusions need not necessarily be false—that is to say, unrealizable or in contradiction to reality.[17]

Freud continues:

> We shall tell ourselves that it would be very nice if there were a God who created the world and was a benevolent Providence, and if there were a moral order in the universe and an after-life; but it is a very striking fact that all this is exactly as we are bound to wish it to be. And it would be more

> remarkable still if our wretched, ignorant and downtrodden ancestors had succeeded in solving all these difficult riddles of the universe.[18]

Death is the most real and certain thing in our world. Childish, primitive, foolish thinking will hardly help us men of today in conquering it.

Please turn to the next page.

5

The Second Death

The pharmacy of Our Lady of Grace at Mariazell (Austria) is right beside the basilica. On a visit to Mariazell you should certainly buy the stomach drops that are available in the pharmacy; I've used them myself and found them helpful. As I can also tell you from personal experience, priests from abroad should tell the sacristan a day ahead that they wish to celebrate Mass at the altar of the miraculous image. This is especially true in the summer months when there is some competition from the pilgrims who want to celebrate there.

If a priest is bringing a group of pilgrims to Mariazell, he had best contact the local authorities in advance and arrange in writing for saying Mass at the altar at a certain time. As far as shelter is concerned, Mariazell has enough hotels, inns, and rooms in private houses, with prices to suit every pocket; there are plenty of suitable restaurants and eating places. In winter you can ski; there is a funicular railway, and you can swim in nearby Lake Erlauf. Travel to Mariazell from Sankt Pölten by the narrow-gauge railway and you will see some beautiful scenery.

I have frequently taken my vacation at Mariazell and read Mass summer and winter at the altar of grace in the basilica as well as at the high altar and various side altars. A beautiful silent Mass, as I whisper my prayers to myself, often without even a server present.

The altar of grace stands beneath a stone baldacchino in the front part of the basilica (built as a Gothic hall-church in the fourteenth century but later expanded and completed in the baroque style). Silver and gold and candlelight bring a warm glow to the statue of our Lady. The statue is not quite eighteen inches tall (late Romanesque, middle of the twelfth century) and represents Mary with the child Jesus. Heavy brocade robes leave only the head free; our Lady wears a crown.

Duke Henry of the house of Eppenstein gave the area around Mariazell to the Benedictines in 1103, and they founded the first settlement there. Under Duke Henry Ladislas of Moravia the Slavic peoples began to go on pilgrimage to Mariazell, while King Louis I of Hungary started the great pilgrimages from that country. Votive gifts from kings and emperors are kept in the sanctuary, in grateful memory of victories won and graces received. The altar of grace is made of silver, and there I read Mass under the eyes of the miraculous image of God's Mother. Hail Mary, full of grace, the Lord is with thee, blessed art thou among women.

In August the Croats from Burgenland (Austria) sing their ancient songs before the miraculous Mother; they have been coming annually for several hundred years, the older women wear the black garments and black kerchief that are part of their native dress. They know by heart many stanzas of the melancholy old songs; they say the rosary and spend almost the whole day in church. (Vacationers and drivers passing through are astonished at the sight of the old Croatian women.) For several days in August the Croatian pilgrims take over Mariazell; you also meet many of them at Lake Erlauf where you can rent a boat and row on the lake. In the evening there is a candlelight procession around the basilica (weather permitting).

As you can see, Mariazell is a place of pilgrimage and favors received.

The oldest places of pilgrimage thus far discovered are on Crete and date from over four thousand years ago. At that time people sought out certain sanctuaries in hope of a cure for illness and infirmity. Professor Leipoldt says in this connection: "In later times such places were to be found almost everywhere in the world." [1]

In Crete, between 2600 and 1445 B.C., the Minoan culture flourished, with palaces, extensive trade, centralized administration, and writing. On Crete, then, there existed a so-called high culture, one of the oldest of all; things are progressing, we are entering into the light of history. The primitive Stone Age is past and people now sleep in beds. In this connection we can speak of a six-thousand-year-long phase in the history of mankind, that is only now ending as mechanized industry becomes widespread. On this point we can take Professor Toynbee's word (we met him in the previous chapter).

In addition to the invention of places for pilgrimage, we owe this long period a number of other things: for example, the world religions and Greek philosophy, hell and the last judgment and eternal life. As far as the stuff in our heads is concerned we're right in our element. Unfortunately, we can't go into all these points in detail, but must mention only the most important matters. (Six thousand years is a long time. Think of all the things we could talk about! But old Seibold must bear in mind that he'll soon be saying farewell to this world—as we've mentioned several times already—and we must not try his patience too much.)

I have not said Mass at Mariazell for several years now.

THE CONSEQUENCES OF ATTACHMENT

At one time, while the Exalted One was staying in the grove at Savatthi, a man lost his only and much loved little son. From then on he gave no thought to work or food, but was constantly going to the cemetery and lamenting: "Where is my little son, my only son?" Finally, he went to the Exalted One, greeted him, and sat down at his side. The Exalted One said to him: "You are not master of your senses; you are

> distraught." "How could I not be distraught? My dear and only little son is dead. Since he died I have given no thought to work or food, but am constantly going to the cemetery and asking, 'Where is my little son, my only son?' "
>
> The Exalted One said: "What do you expect, sir? When a man is attached (*piya*) to something, the result is care, grief, pain, affliction, and despair. These are the consequences of attachment."
>
> The man went off dissatisfied with the words of the Exalted One.[2]

(The translator notes that *piya* means something which is pleasant and which a person wants to have and keep for himself. In the language of Freud we would speak of the object of a narcissistic choice.)

This story comes from the "Middling Collection" of the Buddhist Pali Canon, the collection known as *Majjhima Nikaya*, which was put in writing in Ceylon around the time of Christ's birth, some five hundred years after the death of the Buddha. "Buddha" means the Awakened One and is a title of honor given to the sage Gautama, who was born in Northern India about 560 B.C. as the son of a prince. He was carefully educated, and married a girl of noble family who bore him a son. At the age of twenty-nine Gautama left his family in order to search for salvation as a homeless wanderer. At first he studied the wisdom of the Brahmans; then he spent several years in very strict yoga asceticism, until his health gave way and he became convinced that the method was useless. When he had recovered his strength, he underwent the decisive experience of "awakening." Disciples joined him and together with them he founded the order of the *Sangha* (Community) which still exists. For forty-four years, usually accompanied by a large or small group of disciples, he traveled about Northern India instructing people. At the age of eighty he died in the little town of Kusinara near the Himalayas.

For a long time Buddha's sayings were orally transmitted, but with scrupulous care. This is why each section of the written collection begins with the words: "Thus have I heard it."

Thus have I heard it:

Vacchagotta, the itinerant monk, came to the Exalted One, greeted him courteously, and said: "Is it your opinion that a perfect man lives after death?"

"No."

"Is it your opinion that a perfect man does not live after death?"

"No."

"Is it your opinion that a perfect man both lives and does not live after death?"

"No."

"Is it your opinion that a perfect man neither lives nor does not live after death?"

"No."

Vacchagotta then repeated all the questions and answers, and at the end asked: "Lord Gautama, what is so bad about these opinions that you reject them all?"

The Exalted One answered: "All these theories are a thicket, a wilderness, and inseparable from evils, vexation, confusion, and feverish unrest. They do not lead to release, cessation, pacification, deep knowledge, enlightenment, and nirvana. That is the disadvantage that I see in them, and that is why I reject them all."

"Lord Gautama, do you have any theory at all, then?"

"A man fulfilled has no theories."

Then Vacchagotta repeated all the questions and answers again, and continued: "Now I am ignorant and confused, and the deep sense of satisfaction I derived from earlier conversations with Lord Gautama has disappeared."

The Exalted One replied: "You and your ignorance and confusion, Vaccha! This truth is deep, hard to grasp, and difficult to penetrate; it is calm and glorious; it transcends thought and is most profound, so that only the wise understand it. You cannot grasp it, because you approach it with an outlook alien to it, with an alien way of thinking and under alien influences; your aims are alien to it, and you lead an alien way of life. . . . A perfect man is liberated from a life characterized by the body; he is profound, immeasurable, and incomprehensible, like the great sea. No one can say that he will come again; no one can say that he will not come again; no one can say that he will both come again and not come again; no one can say that he will neither come again nor not come again."

Whereupon Vacchagotta said: "This explanation of Lord Gautama is like a tree which, when the branches have been lopped off and the bark and green wood removed, consists only of heartwood."

Vacchagotta declared himself convinced, took refuge with the Buddha and his teaching and the community of disciples, and became a follower for the rest of his life.[3]

My normal technique of language leaves me.[4] Wittgenstein

From the lectures of Ludwig Wittgenstein on religious belief:

An Austrian general said to someone: "I shall think of you after my death, if that should be possible." We can imagine one group who would find this ludicrous, another who wouldn't. [During the War, Wittgenstein saw consecrated bread being carried in chromium steel. This struck him as ludicrous.]

Suppose that someone believes in the Last Judgment, and I don't, does this mean that I believe the opposite to him, just that there won't be such a thing? I would say: "Not at all, or not always."

Suppose I say that the body will rot, and another says "No. Particles will rejoin in a thousand years, and there will be a Resurrection of you."

If someone said: "Wittgenstein, do you believe in this?" I'd say: "No." "Do you contradict this man?" I'd say: "No."[5]

Gautama Buddha (died ca. 480 B.C.) and Ludwig Wittgenstein (died A.D. 1951) in similar circumstances use the negative in a remarkably similar way. Both men are hard to understand; one must become thoroughly acquainted with them, almost their disciple.

It is recommended that you reread the words of Buddha quoted just above at least once more, and slowly. There is not much written on the subject that is of equal value, still less much that is superior, in the literature of the last six thousand years.

SPECIAL DAYS

Buddha is regarded as founder of one of the so-called world religions, which have put all sorts of ideas about the next world into men's heads and are still actively influencing men today. Before the appearance of the so-called high cultures there were no world religions, and there is evidently a connection between the high cultures and the world religions. Professor Toynbee has a theory on this matter. According to Professor Toynbee's view of universal history, we can distinguish twenty-one social bodies over the last six thousand years, as contrasted with the far more numerous primitive cultures (see the previous chapter). Fourteen of these high cultures have died out; seven are still alive (among them the Western, the Orthodox-Christian, the Islamic, the Indic, and the Far Eastern). Six cultures came into existence without known ancestors: the ancient Egyptiac, the Sumeric, the Chinese, the Minoan (Crete), and the Mayan and the Andean in pre-Columbian South America. All others are, in one or other form, the second- or third-generation descendants of these.[6]

Between the second- and third-generation cultures Professor Toynbee locates what he calls "universal Churches," which arise when "universal states" break down (Christianity in the Roman Empire is an example).[7] In this way he is able to introduce a certain order into the past six thousand years. Western Culture still survives (but it is not in very good condition just now).

The history of man looks different, however, when it is viewed through the eyes of the majority of men, that is, the two-thirds who are illiterate and close to starvation; in other words, when viewed from below, from the vantage point of the conquered. These are the people who play the short game; life is too short to spend it philosophizing. This silent majority has existed throughout the whole six thousand years. Property and education in the high cultures were always the privilege of distinguished minorities: warriors, traders, priests, and nobles, who had time to reflect on the meaning of life; these people also had a fairly long lifespan.

The minority had their deeds and laws recorded on stone so that they should not be forgotten; priests who could write prepared lists of gods and cracked their heads constructing genealogical tables of divine beings. All the royal histories, victory bulletins, decrees, names of kings, liturgical rubrics, epics, philosophies, and books of the dead could be studied only by someone who could read: a Brahman or mandarin or rabbi or cleric. The rest of the people were mute and at most merely listened to the itinerant storytellers or singers, gazed in wonder at processions, visited shrines, and went to the circus and the chariot races. In most cases the silent majority (propertyless and voiceless) can be regarded as simply the object of history, while the active agents of it were few in number and lived at the center of the city. When the masses swarmed from the periphery to the center, it was for a festival or a rebellion. Such occasions as these are special days in the collective consciousness. (Adolf Hitler still knew how to stage such special days.)

Primitives, too, have their special days: seasonal feasts, marriages, funerals, initiations. But this is not the kind of special days we are concerned with here (that kind still exists, even among us). Our interest is rather in the new quality that arises from a factor which did not come into play in earlier times, namely, the greater number of the participants. Primitive societies (very numerous; several thousand still exist), in comparison with the twenty-one civilizations Professor Toynbee lists, are short-lived and limited to small geographical areas, and contain few members. Size and duration, then, distinguish the primitive societies from the so-called high cultures. (Ancient Egypt, for example, lasted about four thousand years.)

Primitives settle outside the great lasting empires, and are also called barbarians. Sometimes they migrate from wilderness and steppe to more fruitful regions. Alaric captured Rome, the Hyksos invaded Egypt, the Achaians conquered Crete. Armed strangers, pouring from ships or riding swift horses and suddenly appearing before the city walls, ruthless, persevering, and disciplined—*they* bring the inhabitants special days! Then a new regime is established amid the debris of the ruined palaces. Silent sectors of the population in a vast kingdom can also turn savage (Professor Toynbee speaks of "internal proletariats"[8]). The blacks in the United States, the Roman slaves in Sicily, the Catholics in Northern Ireland: all make headlines, and people talk of a time of troubles. In any event, all this creates special days.

Royal commissioners visit the village; officials appear with military escorts, as do missionaries and traders (with or without military escorts), tax collectors, sergeant majors (they do need soldiers), and judges. These are indeed special days, as a new decree is read, the mayor is ousted from office, the village undergoes baptism, and the young men are thrust into uniform and marched off.

When seen from below, history loses much of its grandeur. Rome and the emperor are as distant as the heavens are high, and special days are by no means always a blessing—as when soldiers march through the city. "Dawn is here, dawn is here, and lights me to an early death. I must be off to the town, I must, I must—while you, my love, lie here!" Polls taken among the masses of the people show that few are well acquainted with the names of government officials, despite the newspapers and the radio. Will our new masters finally get a road built? Who knows, maybe things will change for the better! The Chinese, from all we hear, are better off now than they used to be. From the thirteenth to the fifteenth centuries Bruges (Belgium) was a rich flourishing city, then the harbor silted up, and from the sixteenth century on the city must be said to have declined. Today many tourists visit it (three stars in the guidebook).

History seen from below is surely enigmatic, and yet also relatively monotonous, as compared with the bird's-eye panoramic view we are given in the philosophy of history. Special days are rather infrequent breaks in the dull sameness of life; there are good times and bad times; now and then a thief is hanged, and then there's a little variety for a change. Death sings its slow song, the standards once carried in victory gather dust in the cathedral (somewhere or other), the names of kings and princes are forgotten. What is left is a common tongue, a knowledge of where the boundaries of one's (native) country lie, resentment at injustice suffered—all this for century after century. The heavy weight of substructures, the slowness of adjustments, the sheer sluggishness of history as it is really lived are taken for granted when seen from below; only the professors can be lively and clever about it.

The norms professors use for deçiding what is important in history are quite different from those of old Seibold. He has stricter criteria, as it were, for what has been really important in the last six thousand years; not much passes the test. Nefretete and Barbarossa are dead and buried; you have to be able to read Aristotle and Descartes before you can say anything further about them; next Sunday is the election for the community council.

AL-KARIAH

In the Name of Allah, the Compassionate, the Merciful:

The Disaster! What is the Disaster?

Would that you knew what the Disaster is!

On that day men shall become like scattered moths and the mountains like tufts of carded wool.

Then he whose scales are heavy shall dwell in bliss; but he whose scales are light, the Abyss shall be his home.

Would that you knew what this is like!

It is a scorching fire.[9]

The one hundred and first sura (section, chapter) of the Koran is entitled *al-Kariah* which is translated as "the fatality" or "the catastrophe." Taken literally, the Arabic word suggests a pounding or striking. The heart beats faster at the thought of the day of judgment; lightning strikes, followed by the thunderbolt. Suddenness, an unforeseen rapid breakdown, as in a heart attack. Terror, in any case. When a new heavenly revelation descends upon the prophet, the camel he is riding sinks to its knees under the force of the truth as it strikes.

"The Resurrection":

In the Name of Allah, the Compassionate, the Merciful:

I swear by the Day of Resurrection, and by the self-reproaching soul!

Does man think We shall never put his bones together again? Indeed, We can remould his very fingers!

Yet man would ever deny what is to come. "When will this be," he asks, "this day of Resurrection?"

But when the sight of mortals is confounded and the moon eclipsed; when sun and moon are brought together—on that day man will ask: "Whither shall I flee?"

No, there shall be no escape. For on that day all shall return to Allah.[10]

Thus speaks the prophet; his name is Muhammad (died A.D. 632) and he founded Islam, the youngest of the great religions (it now has about four hundred million adherents). The oracles we have quoted are among the earliest and most basic. (They do not mean much to present-day Muslims, we are told; other suras have become more popular.) At the beginning of his revelations the prophet's soul was filled with a vision of the end: the destruction of the world and the final judgment. But these paradises and hells were Christian in character; there were certainly Christian believers living in the Arabian Peninsula at the time of Muhammad, and no one today doubts the influence of Christian ideas on the prophet. Muhammad voices a feeling that represents something new of its kind with regard to man's lot in the next world. The idea of a final judgment arose in the Near East, somewhere between Iran and Egypt, in the last millennium before Christ.

Confucius and Lao Tzu, the Buddha, the Jewish prophets, Socrates, and Zoroaster all lived during this final thousand years before the start of the Christian era; a good deal was going on in religion and philosophy. Then came Jesus and Paul, and finally Mani (died A.D. 377; he had a strong but now forgotten influence). Muhammad marks the end of this chapter. Later saints, reformers, and founders of religions will not produce any comparable results. In a certain measure we are still living on the ideas of a few highly gifted men who lived from one and a half to two and a half thousand years ago.

Just where or by whom the final judgment was first excogitated is a matter of debate. Jesus certainly did not invent it, it was already there in his time. It arose rather late among the Jews, only two or three centuries before Christ, and had not become universal during that period. Even today there is a doubt about whether the Last Judgment is a Jewish idea at all; many indications point to ancient Persia as the source. But we have no certain knowledge on the point.

Professor Toynbee: "We catch a glimpse of a society in Syria, in the generation of King Solomon and his contemporary King Hiram, which was just discovering the Atlantic and Indian Oceans and had already discovered the Alphabet."[11]

Thus, in the tenth century before Christ Egypt had grown weak and the World Spirit turned away from Egypt. The World Spirit made its exodus from Egypt and its Books of the Dead, its scarabs and other bits of magic on behalf of the dead. A few centuries later, Mene Tekel, and the handwriting was on the wall for Babylon and Assur, and something new seems to be in the works. The Near East is pregnant with a new world view, but it will take a thousand years for it to come to birth. The old stone-age land of the dead stays firmly fixed in men's heads despite cuneiform writing and the alphabet. It is known as Hades to the Greeks and Sheol to the Jews: "Dead they are, they have no life, shades that cannot rise."[12]

Dry bones first come to life in the prophet Ezekiel, with a hope behind them that only the Jews know:

> The hand of the Lord came upon me, and he led me out in the spirit of the Lord and set me in the center of the plain, which was now filled with bones. He made me walk among them in every direction so that I saw how many they were on the surface of the plain. How dry they were! . . . Thus says the Lord God to these bones: See! I will bring spirit into you, that you may come to life. . . . I prophesied as I had been told, and even as I was prophesying I heard a noise; it was a rattling as the bones came together, bone joining bone. I saw the sinews and the flesh come upon them, and the skin cover them, but there was no spirit in them. . . . I prophesied as he told me, and the spirit came into them; they came alive and stood upright, a vast army. Then he said to me: Son of man, these bones are the whole house of Israel. They have been saying, "Our bones are dried up, our hope is lost, and we are cut off." . . . Thus says the Lord God: O my people, I will open your graves and have you rise from them, and bring you back to the land of Israel.[13]

This is first and foremost a mighty promise to a suffering people. The resurrection is not meant to be an international thing, and there is no thought of a final judgment with everyone rendering an account. But the image is there, and a power behind it; a force is now present that cannot be stemmed: what is not now can yet come to be. The Jews return from their Babylonian exile; they build a new temple. Messiah is coming.

Later, in the Book of Daniel, the scenario is much fuller: "Thrones were set up and the Ancient One took his throne. His clothing was snow bright, and the hair on his head white as wool; his throne was flames of fire. . . . The court was convened, and the books were opened." [14]

Still later, and quite clearly: "Many of those who sleep in the dust of the earth shall awake; some shall live forever, others shall be an everlasting horror and disgrace." [15] Finally, the Book of Revelation, in which appeal is already being made to the words of Jesus, is filled with visions of the world's destruction; the orchestra plays as loud as it can, and all the instruments have a part. Angels blow trumpets, books are opened again, the dead rise up to be judged: "The sea gave up its dead; then death and the nether world gave up their dead. Each person was judged according to his conduct. Then death and the nether world were hurled into the pool of fire, which is the second death; anyone whose name was not found inscribed in the book of the living was hurled into this pool of fire." [16]

Father Celestin Pfaffstaller, pastor at the Church of Our Lady of Consolation in Meran (Province of Bolzano, Italy), who died on September 28, 1816, need not fear the second death. On his tombstone, which is attached to the wall of the church, is written: "His bones here await their joyous resurrection."

RELIGIOUS INSTRUCTION

You said no to hell in front of the television camera; you said no at the right moment, and you deserve a mark of 100 in religion. I saw your face on the screen as schoolgirls were being asked their opinion of a God who punishes and of hell; you were a schoolgirl, and your opinion was also asked. The camera cut to you, there was your face, you thought for a moment and then at the right time remembered the right answer: "On the cross Jesus forgave his tormentors; Jesus will never be angry with me."

You made the right choice between this Jesus and the Jesus of Michelangelo in the Sistine Chapel. You have my hearty congratulations; I hope there are many more girls like you.

Dr. Freud reminds his imaginary interlocutor: "Think of the depressing contrast between the radiant intelligence of a healthy child and the feeble intellectual powers of the average adult." [17]

A further point: Protracting the process of sexual development and bringing religion to bear as early as possible are two chief aims of contemporary pedagogy, are they not? Thus, when the child begins to think, religious doctrines have already become sacrosanct to him. But do you think it contributes very much to strengthening the powers of the mind if so important an area is barred to entry by the threat of hellfire?

The radiant intelligence of at least one healthy child has not been rendered fearful by the catechism! "Many are not asked, and many side with what is false. Therefore: the most important thing to learn is understanding." [18]

The schoolgirl on television said no at the right moment, and yes at the right moment; she would not side with what is false. In this instance, and quite unexpectedly, religious instruction bore satisfying fruit despite the feeble intellectual powers of the average adult (including the teacher of religion). Please applaud! We need have no special worry about this schoolgirl; she'll find the right path.

THE VALE OF TEARS

Back to Mariazell. Vacationers and drivers present there have a chance to hear the *Salve Regina*: "Hail, holy Queen, mother of mercy! Hail, our life, our sweetness, and our hope!" (The *Salve Regina* can be traced back to the twelfth century; there is a dispute about who wrote it.) "To thee we do cry, poor banished children of Eve; to thee do we send up our sighs, mourning and weeping in this vale of tears."

In this case our sighs rise up to the Mother of God. She is addressed as Queen in this medieval prayer, and after this our exile will show us her Son, Jesus, the blessed fruit of her womb. Thus the *Salve Regina.*

The exile, the place of banishment, is earthly life. The departure from the primeval paradise was involuntary; it was the sin of the first human beings that led to their expulsion from their native place. We yearn to go back to it: how short this wretched life is in comparison with eternity! In the blessedness of eternity every tear will be wiped away, and the sighs of afflicted creatures will be heard. The evildoer will finally be punished, and his howls will not disturb the happiness of the saints.

The *Salve Regina* contains the whole popular version of the Christian hope with regard to the next life. But meanwhile that hope had faded, and not only in Bochum (see chapter 2); the professors of history are beginning to be interested in it (wherever the carcass is, there will the vultures gather). For some time now, the *Salve Regina* has been used only infrequently, and in fact many people have simply forgotten how to pray. Now that the believer's sighing to heaven is no longer taken for granted, our interest in the historical causes is awakened; we would like to know the why and wherefore.

The first thing that strikes us is that primitives have no idea of a final judgment. The second is that the idea of a justice that balances things off at the end of time arose in a specific spatiotemporal context: the Near East in the second half of the last millennium before Christ.

Not in Asia, then, nor in the Far East, though high cultures existed there. "The idea that for transitory deeds of transient beings on this earth 'eternal' punishment or rewards in the future could be assigned . . . is for all genuine Asiatic thought absurd, appearing spiritually subaltern" (Weber).[19] We may presume, therefore, that our now triumphant Western civilization originates in notions first conceived in the Near East two and a half millennia ago; among these notions was a new (at that time) way of coming to grips with death.

As for the social conditions and presuppositions behind the new belief in another world, we must note first of all a point of information that applies to all the so-called high cultures: "The segment [of cultural values] which the individual and passive recipient or the active co-builder can comprise in the course of a finite life becomes the more trifling the more differentiated and multiplied the cultural values and the goals for self-perfection become."[20] (Max Weber was not the only one to recognize these relationships. We quote him because he dealt more extensively with the sociology of the world religions than did Marx, who had a keener mind, and more penetratingly than the professors who came after him.)

The vale of tears in the *Salve Regina* is, therefore, not simply a universal reality that has always been, as it were, part of the natural order (ever since man appeared on earth). It expresses, rather, a world view that came into existence only when social conditions in the so-called high cultures were ripe for it. Something had gone wrong while the irrigation ditches were being dug in the valleys of the Nile, the Euphrates, and the Tigris; the masses who slaved at the building of the pyramids wept a new kind of tears and hardly knew they were living in a high culture. The multiplication of cultures profited only a very few people who had meanwhile learned how to exercise power in great kingdoms, with the help of solemnly promulgated laws or of ancient customs such as the caste system in India.

Even the Stone Age Tasaday (see the previous chapter) are in their own way afflicted creatures and have reason to sigh. But what afflicts them are relatively simple things by comparison with the slave laborers of the high cultures: the weather, for example, or a scarcity of food in the rain forest. By contrast, the ancient Egyptian who toiled on the pyramids had not only the prehistoric heat to contend with but a historical problem of a very human, not a natural, kind: While he toiled, others took siestas.

> *Viewed in this way, all "culture" appears as man's emancipation from the organically prescribed cycle of natural life. For this very reason culture's every step forward seems condemned to lead to an ever more devastating senselessness.*[21] Max Weber

---

The question of life's overall meaning and the connected longing for release from all the misery of earthly existence came with this social stratification and the kind of political domination that the so-called high cultures brought with them. The question and the longing were a reaction to the way the pie has been divided ever since the Iron Age. That question about life's meaning has been answered in various ways during the last six thousand years; nothing good is accomplished in haste. It took a rather long time before men began to look differently at what seemed to have developed quite naturally, and to start talking about the vale of tears. It took an even longer time before they asked themselves whether it might not be more practical to change the insupportable conditions instead of looking for new and subtler answers to the meaning of life.

We may safely assert, then, that all the conceptions of the next life (and not just the Last Judgment) which came in with the high cultures are by no means concerned simply with natural death. They are also (and this is important) an answer to the unresolved problems of life that arise whenever the primitive mentality has been left behind by a society as a whole.

Such a collective emergence from the ancient world in which the land of the dead was a matter of experience probably occurred first among the Jews after the Babylonian exile. The step was taken not merely by a few sages, as elsewhere, but by increasingly large sectors of the population as they rebelled against the whole tyranny of the high cultures (upon which the people had already turned their backs under Moses). All sorts of fantasies were invented and elaborated in apocalyptic dream books and in visionary symbols (as in Ezekiel and Daniel), but the central idea was sharp and clear: This world is evil, we want a new heaven and a new earth, we want justice.

We are saying, then, that piety need not always be simply a sigh from the afflicted creature as it is at Mariazell and in the *Salve Regina* and in religion class. It can also turn into protest against the real wretchedness that is manmade. The Last Judgment contains that kind of protest. In it even the flayed body and the body suffering from the denial of its instincts has its rights restored: it will rise from the dead; even in death it will not be forgotten.

However fantastic, useless, or even illusory this outlook may seem today (even Jesus moved within its orbit), the knowledge it manifests of man's world and the radical critique it embodies are something new; men have bidden farewell to the bias imposed by tradition and left behind them the Egyptian fleshpots of the high cultures. The negation of death's finality (in the belief in resurrection and in the expectation of a Last Judgment) has in this instance sharpened men's awareness of circumstances and conditions in a way that is new in principle and has not become outmoded even today.

Thus, even hell can have its good points. The only question is: Who is to be condemned to it?

6

Good Night

In a play written in 1952 and first produced at Oxford in 1956 Elias Canetti deals with the most radical of all the real inequalities between men: their differing lifespans. In this drama he depicts a society in which every individual knows exactly how many years he will live; that number is his name. With this as background he shows how men relate to death. They accept it or secretly rebel against it. But the challenging of this order of things and its overthrow by a rebel only lead to the state of affairs with which we are now familiar. Thus the play brings to light all the attitudes to death that are to be found among men. The title of the piece is *The Deadliners.*[1]

All the attitudes to death that are to be found among men: the number may be set high or low, but in any case the assumption is made that the number of attitudes to death among men is finite, not infinite. The attitudes men have toward death can be counted; they can be inventoried. How high the number may turn out to be (greater or less than a hundred, for example) is a matter for dispute, given the present state of our knowledge. But the determination of the precise number of attitudes toward death is probably of secondary importance. The important thing is the insight that the number is finite. As we shall see, the number is almost surely less than one hundred and very probably less than fifty.

The final words of dying individuals have sometimes been collected and published. One such collection, printed on handmade paper, has seventeen sections, each containing a group of sayings regarded as typical of a given interior attitude.[2] The editor says he does not intend his divisions to represent a complete classification, but simply a provisional overview. It becomes immediately clear that the differences between attitudes toward death are substantial. For example:

Ramón María Narvaez (1800–1868), Duke of Valencia, Marshal, Prime Minister, to his confessor: "I have no need to forgive my enemies, since I've done away with all of them."

Josephte Brillat-Savarin (1757–1855), sister of the famous writer on gastronomy, was about to finish her dinner in bed when she felt suddenly weak and cried out: "I feel the end is near! The dessert, quickly!"

Winston Churchill (1874–1965): "It is all so boring."

Jakob Boehme (1575–1624), Protestant mystic and visionary: "Now I take my journey to Paradise!"

Thomas Mann (1875–1955), writer: "Give me my glasses!"

Thomas Edison (1847–1931), American inventor, as he awakened from a deep coma for the last time: "It is very beautiful here on the other side."

Matthias Claudius (1740–1815), writer: "Good night!"

CONVERSATIONS WITH EVELINA

There have been philosophers for the last two and a half millennia; the man usually regarded as the first was Thales of Miletus, who lived in the sixth century B.C. in Ionia (west coast of modern Turkey). Philosophers are solitary people, though sometimes a few students seek their company. Philosophers are hard to understand and therefore have a rather small public, yet many of their ideas prove surprisingly durable and last for many centuries. For some time now many philosophers have also been professors

(Kant and Hegel, for example); many others, on the contrary, do their thinking in private (Kierkegaard, for example). Philosophers have thought about death and have come up with different answers; it is difficult to ascertain the precise number of philosophical ideas about death. In our own century Martin Heidegger especially has come forward with thoughts on death in his book *Being and Time.*[3]

Evelina Krieger (Doctor of Philosophy) did not come forward; she did not become famous like Martin Heidegger, but died at thirty-five before achieving philosophical renown. It is now time to speak of Evelina in connection with philosophy and death. Evelina was a woman of great philosophical gifts; she published books and essays in the professional journals, but never became a professor or even an assistant at the university, and therefore remained poor all her life. Until she was thirty she did have a small pension because of her father, a Jew who had had to flee under Hitler and died abroad; once she was thirty the reparations pension stopped. For two years she had a scholarship; after that she lived from hand to mouth; her mother had no property at all.

Evelina had a sweetheart, a priest bound to celibacy; she was willing to respect that fact and remain chaste like him. In conversations with Evelina his name often came up; he had turned from her, but she was unwilling to let him go, she had her heart set on him; later, he left his Order and married someone else. How is this kind of suffering to be handled philosophically? In her first book Evelina answered: "without you there is no meaning."[4]

In conversations with Evelina she spoke of her fits of utter dejection. She suffered from depression: when she awoke in the morning, she had to spend an hour in bed weeping, only then could she get up. She knew perfectly well that she suffered from depression; she was shrewd enough to realize that her suffering was a psychic illness, but the knowledge didn't lessen the suffering. In her letters she longed for affection and security: without you there is no meaning.

Evelina to me:[5]

Please love me, please love me awfully much. I always have this terrible fear that the people close to me may suddenly turn into green masks with huge hostile mouths, the way I see them in dreams when I have a fever. Dear people very close to me suddenly become quite reserved and I don't know why; if I ask them, it only makes matters worse. You yourself have acted that way many a time, but I know it was just a reaction of fear at being loved, I'm sure of that. But now you've lost that fear and even on the telephone you've been very loving to me for years now. Please be that way always! If you only knew how it helps me to be loved!—you know the kind of love I mean: always even, not disappointing the other over long, long periods, protective, always the same. I think that's the only thing that can help me.

From Rome:

I've just spent another night in mortal terror. Then I went to the kitchen and swilled wine; then I was able to sleep. I am shattered. In the night the devil appears to me as the more powerful god. During the day I know only that I am lost, but I'm not in hell yet. If only we still lived among the ruins of the ancient temples, with the lizards and the sun and the gods and the sea—how beautiful that would be!

From Palermo:

Here I am in Palermo, and filled with an awful longing for God. He is so far, far, far distant from our lives. Why can't we see him face to face in this life even for a single fleeting moment? I'd give my life for that! I'm busy writing the lecture for ——— and working on the conclusion of the article for ———. Do you think that at least the dear Lord is satisfied with me? If he were, then I could bear the emptiness.

Evelina is courageous; her longing for God is a terrible thing. She writes philosophical lectures and articles and reviews without stopping, until she is exhausted. Frequent migraines and a bone-marrow suppuration that reappears from time to time cause her great concern. She conducts a running discussion with Hegel in her writings; she masters the dialectic and writes difficult sentences like this one: "Death is the passage from my immediacy as simple finitude to my proper meaning in which my finitude persists but now as a gift to me." [6]

I tell Evelina she should write more intelligible sentences. She likes to come to my Mass now and then; I give her the host on these occasions and she renews her courage: "I'll have no second chance."

Conversations with Evelina yield a lesson that is as bitter as death itself. Neither Thales of Miletus nor Martin Heidegger were of any great help to philosopher Evelina Krieger in her suffering and death, nor were Kant and Hegel or Thomas Aquinas. Philosophical ideas of death all proved inadequate for Evelina Krieger's problem. She read an awful lot of philosophy and theology and herself pursued the truth as a highly talented philosopher and theologian, but the devil was stronger and God was so far away. (Even Dr. Freud probably couldn't have helped her.) In the last analysis I couldn't help her either, but I did have something to offer that was important to her and helped her. Here, for the first time, we turn in utmost seriousness to Jesus Christ. The decisive thing here is not whether we come up with some new ideas about Jesus; the important thing is that we have someone about whom we can (should) get new ideas. This is not a matter to be treated lightly.

Still less important, and indeed entirely insignificant in this context, is the question whether it is even possible to get any new ideas about death. So many ideas have already been thought up by those who are skilled in thinking up new ideas; along with Western philosophy we have the worlds of Chinese and Indian thought. In this wide universe of ideas there should have been at least one thought that could have solved Evelina's problem, but there wasn't, and so we are able to state one solid conclusion:

Good Night

Thinking solves no problems, least of all the problem of death.

INVENTORY OF BELIEFS

The relationships of men to death, as a subject of scientific study, fall within that part of psychology that deals with opinions, attitudes, and beliefs. The handbook of Berelson and Steiner uses the acronym OAB.[7] The terminology is still fluid; sometimes people speak of value judgments. Within the realm of OAB a broad division can be made in terms of the intensity and stability of the judgments in question. Thus, opinions are the weakest in intensity and change the quickest (for example, opinions about fashion); beliefs, on the contrary, are very constant and are surrendered only with great reluctance (think, for example, of attitudes to abortion); attitudes, according to these criteria, fit somewhere between opinions and beliefs.

Professor Morris acknowledges that as a philosopher he has been influenced by American pragmatism (Peirce, James, Dewey, Mead, Lewis). In 1945 he began a study the results of which were published in 1956: *Varieties of Human Value.*[8] Here he presents thirteen "ways to live." In an earlier work Professor Morris had attempted an inventory of religious attitudes and ethical systems; after the War he proceeded to test his data scientifically with the help of psychological methods. People filled out his questionnaires not only in the United States but in India, China, Japan, Italy, and Norway as well. The answers were subjected to what is called factor analysis. Five factors, or "dimensions," emerged. Professor Morris has created a five-dimensional attitudinal space, in which the various world views and beliefs are located and can be readily surveyed. In this case American pragmatism confirms something old Lao Tzu once said (in a saying Professor Morris uses as a motto for his book): "In the affairs of men there is a system."

Professor Bales has made his name chiefly through the study of small groups. He too was interested in value statements, because the individuals he tested in laboratory groups produced such statements in abundance; the professor needed some kind of overview of them all. He too had a practical research project, and in his researches he was able to make use of Professor Morris' work as well as the work of many other scholars (Allport, Vernon, Lindzey, Kluckholm, Winter, Sorokin, Adorno, Levinson, Sanford, Couch-Goodrich, Jones, Murray, Cattell, Thurstone).

Professor Bales and his team endeavored, first of all, to collect as many and varied assertions as possible that could be regarded as, in one way or another, value judgments. They gathered 872 such statements, reduced them to 252, and made them the basis of a questionnaire (532 respondents; seven categories of answers, ranging from "disagree completely" to "agree completely"). After some further propositions had been eliminated as irrelevant, the remaining 143 value judgments and the reactions of the respondents were submitted to a factor analysis which yielded four factors (or dimensions; see above).

Professor Bales and Professor Morris conferred and concluded that despite the difference in the number of factors each had found, their results were pretty much in agreement; the difference in the number of factors could be explained by the different statistical techniques they had used.

According to Professor Bales, then, there are four basic dimensions in the world of value statements; these dimensions define an attitudinal space, or value space as Professor Bales calls it, and a whole range of human value judgments can be located within it, including value judgments relative to death.[9] We shall give a very brief, simplified description of Professor Bales's four dimensions.

Factor I relates to authoritarianism; typical statement: "Obedience and respect for authority are the most important virtues children should learn." Factor II relates to self-expression and gratification; typical statement: "Let us eat, drink, and be merry, for tomorrow we die!" Factor III relates to readiness to cooperate; typical statement: "Everyone should have an equal chance and an equal say." Factor IV relates to individualism; typical statement: "It is the man who stands alone who excites our admiration."

The four dimensions can also be regarded as measurements (like length, breadth, and height); this means they are independent of each other and can be combined in many ways. It is not at all true that a strongly authoritarian person must be opposed to sense gratification; the contrary also occurs. Similarly, readiness to cooperate does not exclude individualism, nor sensuality cooperativeness, etc. The important point is that there is a limited number of dimensions; any beliefs whatsoever can be regarded as points in a four-dimensional space that is defined by the factors indicated above. It is conceivable that further research along the same lines would uncover hitherto unknown attitudinal dimensions. But, as we said earlier, we human beings have only a limited number of conceptions of life and attitudes to death, and the four dimensions are quite enough for the time being.

An example: Ten people gather at a hotel for a weekend or for their two weeks' vacation; one evening the conversation turns to basic attitudes toward life.[10] During the discussion one person expresses the following convictions: "Man can solve all his important problems without help from a Supreme Being"—"Heaven and Hell are products of man's imagination, and do not actually exist"—"Christianity and all other religions are, at best, only partly true."

Another disagrees strongly with such views: "Life would hardly be worth living without the promise of immortality and life after death"—"The chief end of man is nothing other than eternal salvation"—"Theology will ultimately prove more important for mankind than the sciences."

A third: "Every person has a set time to live, and when his time comes to die, there is nothing he can do about it"—"It is useless to quarrel with destiny"—"A person should let himself be molded by the great objective purposes of the universe which silently and irresistibly achieve their goal."

And so forth; we won't bother with the other seven participants. The statements quoted are taken from Professor Bales's questionnaire which contains, as we mentioned, 143 such statements of attitudes and convictions; we need not list them all here. It is far more interesting to note that our three fictive participants in the conversation represent types. According to Professor Bales, the first is a B-type, the second an F-type, and the third a UNF-type.

Professor Bales has turned up 35 types and assigned each one or more letters by way of a name. In addition, he has tried to connect each of the 143 statements in his questionnaire with one of the 35 types. The results (as applied to our three examples) look something like this:

The person who denies heaven and hell, is a skeptic about religion, and intends to run his life without God (B-type) also favors radical changes in society; he is clearly opposed to the values measured by Factor I, that is, to authoritarianism. He rejects the conservative beliefs voiced by others in the group.

His opposite in the group (the F-type) is a conservative; he does not wish to disturb the existing beliefs of the members of the group, as Mr. B does; he is rather reserved about self-expression and gratification (Factor II), and authority is important to him. In the religious sphere he holds the traditional belief in a life after death, and is skeptical about modern science.

The third man (or woman) is a domineering person; he is stoic or fatalistic about death, lays great stress on obedience. He becomes the center of the value conflicts that emerge in the group; he'd like nothing better than to punish those opposed to him (like Mr. B), and has to hold himself very much in check if he is not to appear much too aggressive. It would be prudent to think twice before sharing a vacation with Mr. or Ms. UNF.

Thus far our example.

Professor Bales needs 187 pages of fairly small print to describe the 35 types and their respective beliefs, and even a very abbreviated summary would be wearisome. It might be interesting to make a parlor game for six people out of some of the main types Professor Bales shows us.[11] Each player is given a set of cards on which are printed the value judgments and beliefs which he has to represent in the game. The first player represents power and the striving for success; the second is the cooperative man; the third is the conservative; the fourth is the individualist loner; the fifth embraces all traditional values; and the sixth mocks everything, even himself.

The one who gets the highest throw of the dice begins. He takes the first card from his pack, reads it aloud to the others, and then throws the card into a box at the center of the table. The dice are thrown again (it's best to use three dice); the winner reads a card, throws it into the box, and so on. The first one to get rid of all his cards is the winner. To add interest to the game, you can play a tape recorder throughout and thus preserve everything the players say. You'll be surprised, when you play the tape back, at how moving an experience it is to listen to a public discussion of the ways in which people view the world.

The disadvantage of the game is that it will probably become boring rather quickly. Real life is much more varied; the newspapers are filled with differences of opinion, and there are many possible combinations and nuances, probably even more than Professor Bales's 35. (Think of the many religious sects in Great Britain and the United States.) The important thing is that the number of beliefs is limited even when you take into account all the possible ways of combining the principal or basic orientations. In practice it is advisable to neglect insignificant variations of beliefs and to hold to Professor Bales's 35 types, especially since this makes it possible to get some grasp of the subject as a whole.

Unlike the parlor game we have described and unlike the procedures in Professor Bales's laboratory for the study of groups, real life has a basic rule that is unfortunately quite often forgotten in the debate over world views: All participants must die. When this is kept in mind, all beliefs become equally valid, since death asks no one about his opinions. We cannot but think that beliefs cannot resolve the problem of death.

WHY IN ZÜRICH?

A tour of the world of ideas and beliefs can be likened to a visit to a library. Robert Musil has described such a visit, with forceful irony, in the one hundredth chapter of his novel *The Man Without Qualities* (title of chapter: "General Stumm invades the State Library and gathers some experience with regard to librarians, library attendants, and intellectual order").[12] And in fact, when we walk through the library of mankind's ideas about death it is difficult to suppress a strong feeling of "Who's going to read all this?" In this awkward situation General Stumm turns to the librarian and tells him what he wants:

> "For instance, a compendium of all great humanitarian ideas—was there," I asked him cunningly, "anything like that?" . . .
>
> "Or a book on the realization of the quintessential?" I asked.
>
> "Ah, something on theological ethics?" he suggested.
>
> "By all means theological ethics, if you like, but" I insisted, "there must be something in it about good old Austrian culture and a bit about Grillparzer." [13]

General Stumm really wants "some sort of railway time-table that would make it possible to get cross-connections between ideas going in every direction." [14] Such a time-table doesn't exist as yet. General Stumm nonetheless makes an important discovery on his visit to the library; he comes to understand "why in the army where we have the highest degree of order, we also have to be prepared to lay down our lives at any moment. . . . At a certain stage order somehow creates a demand for bloodshed." [15]

(Old Seibold must forgive us for making such a hasty tour of mankind's great ideas that the ideas are not being presented in an orderly fashion.)

The sheer abundance of great ideas and beliefs is bewildering in any event ("You and your ignorance and confusion, Vaccha!" says the Buddha with a gentle smile; see the previous chapter), even though their number is finite.

Not all ideas are great ideas, however. There are also little ideas that haven't met with success or been greeted with widespread public and even official respect, like those of Kant and Hegel. The little ideas have their day rather in small groups and clubs and conventicles, or frequently find only a single person to take them seriously (their author, who cannot find a publisher). But the little ideas should not a priori be assumed to be any less true than the big ideas, just because they do not gain recognition and wide dissemination.

There is no general acknowledgment that personal survival after death has long since been scientifically proved. Therefore we call this one of mankind's little ideas; it is maintained by Professor Hinz of Göttingen in his book *Security.*[16]

Professor Hinz:

> My experiences and observations relate especially to Beatrice Brunner, a medium who speaks in a deep trance. Since 1948 she has been mediator with the world of higher spirits at the Spirit Lodge of Zürich (secretarial office: Münchhaldenstrasse 9, CH 8008 Zürich). Around 8:00 P.M. each Saturday she comes before the public on the stage of the Zürich Conservatory of Music. She sits down and prays silently; with any cooperation from the audience she then falls almost imperceptibly into a deep trance as soon as the music stops; her condition can be recognized only by the fact that with closed mouth she suddenly draws a deep breath and her upper body grows rigid. Immediately thereupon, the words "Praise God" are spoken through her by a spirit who calls himself Joseph

> for the sake of his human audience. As spiritual teacher of the Spirit Lodge, Joseph has delivered well over a thousand lectures of more than an hour's length each. These have been recorded on tape and are now in print (*Messages from the Other World*, three handsome volumes obtainable from the secretarial office, 15 Swiss francs each). When the religious lecture is over, the spirit Joseph bids his hearers farewell using the same words with which he began, and Beatrice the medium awakens with a deep exhalation.[17]

Professor Hinz, after a critical examination of the messages, says: "I speak as a scientist when I tell you, as seriously and emphatically as I can, that these are communications from a higher world. They are revelations by God's messengers in our time."

To the question why Zürich should be the place where such messages from higher worlds reach us men, Professor Hinz replies that communication with the world of the divine is possible when, first of all, a medium strives upward with all of his or her moral powers, and when, secondly, the community in which the medium works, also turns its thoughts to heaven and thus creates an elevated religious atmosphere in which God's messengers can make their presence known. Both conditions are fulfilled at the Spirit Lodge of Zürich and in medium Beatrice as well as in the other mediums of the community. To take part in a service there is to understand what the services of the first Christians at the beginning of the Church must have been like.

Thus far Professor Hinz with regard to Zürich.

His book also contains many interesting details about the experiences of the dead in the other world: they are well off there, there is no hell.

For example:

> It's better here than on earth; it's warm, and nothing is comparable to what you experience there on earth. There are angels; I have a friend among them, a big fellow, and I live in

> a tower. There's no noise here, just melodious sounds. If only I could take you around this fairy world! Bach's music is congenial to our wonderful world here; it is in harmony with heaven. To you this conversation seems abstract, since you can't hear or see me, and you can hardly tell whether your thoughts come from yourself or are infused into you from a higher world. But how could such an abundance of pure conceptions arise in you from yourself? "They come from the unconscious," the skeptic will say. But why should the skeptic be right, rather than I who say to you: "Mama, it's your son who tells you the things you're writing down"? [18]

Roland de Jouvenal, who died at Paris on May 2, 1946, at the age of fifteen, guides the hand of his mother, Marcelle (Professor Hinz calls this "writing from a distance"); she publishes these messages later on, and Professor Hinz now quotes from the French original. There is also a German edition with a preface by the well-known philosopher Gabriel Marcel who states therein that he believes in the truth of what is said in the book. Catholics may read the book without spiritual harm, since it has the imprimatur of the see of Basel.

An ecclesiastical imprimatur and the support of a well-known philosopher help Roland dispel doubts about his genuineness; they are proof that he comes not from his mother's unconscious but from the other world where it is warm. Besides, what does Dr. Freud know of the other world? At least, he hasn't sent any messages so far.

Professor Hinz values his references (the Catholic Church, the well-known philosopher); he speaks emphatically as a scientist with academic standing. He knows that in this scientific, technological age there are many skeptics; he wants to rouse his hearers to faith and knows that without authority there can be no faith. Aurelius Augustine was aware of this a long time ago. In his day the authority was called the *Catholica* (see chapter 2), and men could appeal to it for a thousand years to come, but today it's pretty much a thing of the past. In those days ideas about the other world were great ideas, generally accepted ideas. Today that's no longer so (Bochum!). But Professor Hinz wants to make the ideas he defends become great ideas once again; Gabriel Marcel and the Catholic Church are to help him, as is modern science. But Professor Hinz labors under a handicap: the wider public is skeptical and antecedently distrustful of messages from the other world.

No one believes anything unless he is first convinced it is to be believed.[19]

Augustine

But the conviction doesn't arise at will; it is supported by social consensus. Four hundred years ago belief in witches was taken for granted; this made it a matter of life and death for many. In old prayerbooks we find eyewitness reports from the other world similar to those recounted by Professor Hinz, except that they were much more sensuous and terrifying, untransfigured as it were. For example, in *The Key to Heaven* of the Capuchin preacher Martin von Cochem (imprimatur 1691), the poor souls in purgatory are still being eaten by worms and bathed in sweat, according to authentic tradition and the reliable testimony of an English monk who "in spirit was taken to Purgatory for three days and saw fearful things."[20] Today, purgatory has become a dull affair, rather stale and insipid, and even the Catholic hell lost a lot of its terror during the Enlightenment.[21]

Even beliefs, then, have their ups and downs. Professor Hinz does not have an easy time of it with his revelations from Zürich. Spirit Joseph and Roland de Jouvenal have so far not been able to win general acceptance and, despite the ecclesiastical imprimatur, are relegated to the realm of parapsychology.

In the scientific, technological age only one authority is universally accepted by communists and capitalists alike as the modern equivalent of the *Catholica*, and that authority is science. Anything presented in the guise of science has antecedently a good chance of being regarded by the wider public as credible. Even ordinary inoffensive mineral waters come togged out in scientific garb and adorned with expert opinions and chemical analyses. The method is effective in winning confidence; people prefer to drink scientifically tested mineral water rather than unscientific beverages; faith is at work. (Faith and trust go together, as we read in Dr. Luther.)

Spirits that have not passed the scientific test have, for about the last hundred years, been assigned to parapsychology. (An M. Dessoir suggested the name parapsychology in 1886.) Today this discipline has already gained acceptance in the universities, where its fields of research cover "extrasensory perception," "psychokinetics," and similar matters. Professor Rhine (United States) has suggested that the phenomena in question are to be connected with a basic psychic function known simply as PSI.[22] It does not bother the scientists that little is yet known of this PSI function. They continue cheerfully with their researches, busy themselves with telepathy and clairvoyance, work with mediums in trances; even the military has now gotten interested in certain phenomena of this kind.

All of this has nothing to do with the other world but is simply the study of hitherto unexplained psychic powers; in fifty or a hundred years we may be better informed about them. Precognitions of death, poltergeists and trances, spiritualist seances and mental telepathy won't take us back to the lost paradise of the human race; at least they won't take most people back, since even in Zürich their first allegiance is to science. Beatrice the medium and Joseph the spirit are dubious figures to the scientific world, and Professor Hinz's views make him almost a loner in parapsychology; the latter is indifferent to the garden of Eden and spends its time, in good scientific fashion, on numbers and measurements. Universities and research institutes do not provide inner security, as Professor Hinz does; their business is knowledge, not comfort.

Modern science offers no comfort: when the brain stops functioning, consciousness vanishes; if no brain function, then no consciousness, no spirits, no astral bodies. Science is much grieved to say it, but unfortunately brain cells deteriorate very rapidly without a supply of blood; in a couple of minutes, it's all over. Good night.

7

No More Latin

Dear Mr. Seibold,

In your letter you asked me a question: "What does, or doesn't, come after death?" Please don't be annoyed with me for making you wait so long for an answer. I could, of course, have referred you to the teachings of the Church to which we both belong; they can be found in any catechism, usually under the heading "The Last Things." But I thought it clear from your letter that these teachings do not seem to mean much to you any more, at least in the form in which they were given to you long ago.

This is why I thought it appropriate to make a sort of tour through those customs and ideas of mankind that are somehow related to death. The tour is now finished. I'm probably not far off the mark in assuming that you don't find the results of the survey especially encouraging or consoling. I feel the same way, and, if all indications are not misleading, we're not alone in our uneasiness.

The confidence you've placed in me embarrasses me as much as it honors me. For, I see myself now forced to admit that I cannot give a conclusive answer to your question.

This does not mean, of course, that a conclusive answer does not exist. All it means is that *I* don't know it. Perhaps you'll think that I'm taking my incompetence rather lightly. Not so: for more than twenty years my profession has required me to deal mainly with philosophical and theological questions, the last ten years as a professor. I also have a general knowledge of the historical and social sciences. The tour I've conducted thus represents a summary of the relevant material I've mastered in the course of time. A very personal summary, undoubtedly, but it was the only kind of presentation I could make.

Perhaps some unknown Indian master answered your question many centuries ago; perhaps the answer is to be found in the writings of some forgotten German mystic of the Middle Ages or in the teachings of the Rosicrucians. Frankly, I don't think so, although the gaps in my knowledge are undoubtedly extensive.

The occasion for your letter was my most recent book (the one on Jesus). You say that the Jesus I portrayed pleased you. Yet you asked your question, and now we are both of us no wiser than we were before.

In today's newspaper[1] I saw a full-page advertisement for the advertising agency of Ogilvy and Mather. It contains twenty-eight guidelines for all who wish to compose or evaluate an advertisement; these guidelines are from the pen of Mr. Ogilvy himself. There is one principle he enunciates that I must not deprive you of; it says: "It is better to know than to believe."

The proposition really says very little, it seems to me, and it is no better when reversed. Even Mr. Ogilvy puts it down rather in passing; he is simply emphasizing the need of scientific analyses. Mr. Ogilvy has emerged victorious in the centuries-long struggle between knowing and believing. The victory is complete, taken-for-granted, and irreversible; it need not be especially stressed, it is enough to mention it in passing.

The harshness with which modern economics, modern science, and modern technology dismiss your problem, and the consequent offhandedness with which they treat all ultimate questions are typical of the present situation in which I find myself unable to answer your question. Your question must remain unanswered—and this observation also contains my answer to you.

But I am anticipating. Meanwhile, though I am in no position to give you a conclusive answer, I want you to know that I do appreciate the urgency of your question. My privileged position as a writer (good with words, as you put it in your letter) will be of some use to you by encouraging in people that sharp eye for human concerns that is required if we are to face the problem of death in an unaffected way. Undoubtedly I cannot by writing bring about a state of affairs in our society that will cause the problem of death to disappear. But I can at least attempt to write in such a way that "consummate negativity, once squarely faced, [will] delineate the mirror-image of its opposite." (The words are from Theodor W. Adorno.)[2]

As you know, I am not a purely private individual. I have adhered to a historical force in which I can recognize myself, because it is the power of a principle of negativity and self-criticism. The palpable forms this historical force has taken are today in decline—both the ecclesiastical institutions and the beliefs that accompany them. Yet that force itself is by no means spent as far as I am concerned: I know that it still impels me, and I belong among those who participate in it. Consequently, my aim here is not to put clever ideas on paper in that undisciplined, offhand manner that now characterizes what we like to call our intellectual life. Rather do I see myself, when confronted with the unresolved problem of death (see above), impelled to track down the hints of a possible hope. (Jesus has left such hints behind him.)

There is a story in the Bible which, I think, expresses more concretely what I have just been saying. I shall therefore quote it to you:

> When our fathers were being exiled to Persia, devout priests of the time took some of the fire from the altar and hid it secretly in the hollow of a dry cistern, making sure that the place would be unknown to anyone. Many years later, when it so pleased God, Nehemiah, commissioned by the king of Persia, sent the descendants of the priests who had hidden the

> fire to look for it. When they informed us that they could not find any fire, but only muddy water, he ordered them to scoop some out and bring it. After the material for the sacrifice had been prepared, Nehemiah ordered the priests to sprinkle with the water the wood and what lay on it. When this was done and in time the sun, which had been clouded over, began to shine, a great fire blazed up, so that everyone marveled.[3]

I like this story, and I hope it appeals to you as well.

In one of your most recent letters[4] you write:

> Are we redeemed? From what do we men want to be redeemed while we are on earth? From want, hunger, sickness, distress, and death. Are we redeemed from these? The Church says: Christ has redeemed us from our sins. From what sins? And sins have a cause. Why aren't we redeemed from these causes as well? Perhaps all this stuff that I write seems stupid to you, because I've stayed with the cathechism I learned in grade school. I was forced to become a farmer who couldn't get any further education, and have always had to rely on my own resources in thinking and acting.

A wiser man than I, Theodor W. Adorno (philosopher; died 1970), wrote the following:

> The only philosophy which can be responsibly practised in the face of despair is the attempt to contemplate all things as they would present themselves from the standpoint of redemption. Knowledge has no light but that shed on the world by redemption: all else is reconstruction, mere technique. Perspectives must be fashioned that displace and estrange the world, reveal it to be, with its rifts and crevices, as indigent and distorted as it will appear one day in the messianic light.[5]

Shall I say: "Yes, we are redeemed"—when every second a man somewhere in the world dies of hunger?

Shall I say: "No, we are not redeemed"—and thus deny the historical force of which I have spoken?

The question of redemption evidently cannot be answered with a yes or a no, nor can the question of what happens after death. We continue to need redemption, and we are impelled to think redemption possible despite all disappointments.

In other words: The Kingdom of God is not to be proved or disproved with a yes or a no; it must be established. The Bible has the beautiful sentence: "This day you will be with me in paradise."[6]

We funeral directors, priests, and philosophers must be more cautious about what we say.

Cordial greetings and best wishes.

RELIGIOUS INSTRUCTION (CONTINUED)

Let me tell you briefly what the Latin is that we are finished with. I will limit myself to the *Fundamentals of Catholic Dogma* by Professor Ott (first edition, 1952, which is the one I studied; later editions contain no new dogmas).[7] The questions that concern us are handled in Book Five which bears the subtitle "The Doctrine of the Last Things or of the Consummation (Eschatology)":

Chapter 1: The Eschatology of the Individual Human Being

1. Death
2. The Particular Judgment
3. Heaven
4. Hell
5. Purgatory

Chapter 2: The Eschatology of the Whole of Humanity

6. The Second Coming of Christ
7. The Resurrection of the Dead
8. The General Judgment
9. The End of the World

The following propositions of faith belong, according to Professor Ott, to the fundamentals of Catholic dogma: In the present order of salvation death is a punishment in consequence of sin.—All human beings subject to original sin are subject to the law of death.—Immediately after death the particular judgment takes place, in which, by a Divine Sentence of Judgment, the eternal fate of the deceased person is decided.—The souls of the just, which in the moment of death are free from all guilt of sin and punishment for sin, enter into Heaven.—The blessedness of Heaven lasts for all eternity.—The degree of perfection of the beatific vision is proportioned to each one's merits.—The souls of those who die in the condition of personal grievous sin enter Hell.—The punishment of Hell lasts for all eternity.—The souls of the just which, in the moment of death, are burdened with venial sins and temporal punishment due to sins, enter Purgatory.—At the end of the world Christ will come again in glory to pronounce judgment.—All the dead will rise again on the last day with their bodies.—The dead will rise again with the same bodies as they had on earth.—Christ, on His second coming, will judge all men.—The present world will be destroyed and restored on the Last Day.

In his presentation Professor Ott follows the universally used procedure that has been traditional among teachers of Catholic dogma. First, he states the proposition of faith (in heavy print) and cites the more important decrees of the Councils (there were twenty of these when Ott wrote) on which the dogma is based. Then he gives the "proof from Scripture," that is, adduces the biblical texts which relate to the dogma in question. Last comes the "proof from tradition," which cites various statements of the Church Fathers and theologians on the subject.

Jesus is thus one of many sources in Professor Ott's book: first the dogma (heavy print), then the Councils, then Jesus is permitted to speak, frequently in curtailed form (and in ordinary print).

For example:

> Jesus threatens sinners with the punishment of hell. He calls it Gehenna (Mt. 5, 29 et seq.; 10, 28; 23, 15. 33; Mk. 9, 43. 45. 47 originally = valley of Hinnom), Hell of the fire (Mt. 5, 22; 18, 9), Hell where the worm does not die and the fire is not extinguished (Mk. 9, 46 et seq.), everlasting fire (Mt. 25, 41), unquenchable fire (Mt. 3, 12; Mk. 9, 42), furnace of fire (Mt. 13, 42. 50), everlasting pain (Mt. 25, 46). There will be darkness there (Mt. 8, 12; 22, 13; 25, 30), wailing and gnashing of teeth (Mt. 13, 42. 50; 24, 51; Lk 13, 28)

and so on. (Mt. = Gospel of Matthew, Mk. = Gospel of Mark, Lk. = Gospel of Luke; Gehenna is not mentioned in the Gospel of John.) Professor Ott has worked carefully and is master of his subject. (The material object of theology is God first of all and secondarily created things insofar as they are related to God; Professor Ott here cites Thomas Aquinas.)

Until a few decades ago, lectures in dogmatic theology at the Catholic universities and faculties and academies were given exclusively in Latin.

For the general Catholic public teaching had to be given in a simpler form: through prayers and hymns, pilgrimages and processions, sermons and lessons in school. (In Austria today, during their years of schooling almost all children receive about 640 hours of religious instruction in all.)

At Mariazell (see chapter 5), you may visit the "Mechanical Crèche." It is easily reached in a half hour's walk and lies at a higher level than the shrine itself (splendid view). The mechanical crèche extends over a fairly large area; many figures hardly as big as a man's hand represent the birth of Christ and the important events of his life. Insert a coin and the mechanism starts: the three kings approach the manger, the Samaritan woman draws water from Jacob's Well, Jesus arises from the tomb and quickly ascends, then is taken behind the tiny walls of the tomb and comes forth again.

Visitors usually keep the mechanism going so that they can watch the various scenes at leisure. If there are only a few visitors present and no one is talking, you can hear the noise of the machinery. It knocks and creaks and scrapes like dwarves down in a mine; children especially are impressed. The doors of the tomb open outward, Jesus emerges, and the doors slam shut. After a while even the children have had enough and move on.

The machinery remains silent, people go off for coffee.

PASCAL'S WAGER

At the so-called threshold of modern times a Catholic mathematician jotted down his thoughts on scraps of paper; Blaise Pascal (1623–1662) intended to write a book on the consoling truth of the Christian religion. After his death the fragmentary pieces were collected and published under the title of *Pensées* (*Thoughts*). (Careful! Thinking solves no problems—see the previous chapter.) Pascal built an adding machine, discovered the calculus of probabilities, and worked on the cycloid (a cycloid is a curve generated by a point on the circumference of a rolling circle). At the age of sixteen he wrote an essay on conics in which he developed a theory, named after him, on the hexagon. In 1647 he discovered "Pascal's Law" in hydrostatics and the existence of atmospheric pressure. He also invented a method of calculating (Pascal's Triangle) that became famous.

1654 brought an inner change of direction for the thirty-one-year-old Pascal. In the summer of that year he had presented two treatises to one of the Parisian academies. One night in late autumn God laid hold of him. Not the God of the philosophers and scholars, as he writes on the scrap of paper that later became famous, but the God of Abraham, Isaac, and Joseph, the God of Jesus Christ. (Pascal wrote down the thoughts that moved him so deeply that night and sewed this important memorandum into the lining of his coat.) The decisive thing for this man who was a contemporary of Montaigne and the dawning Enlightenment was: "Certainty, certainty."

Certainty in every matter if possible—that is the basic thing for Pascal: "I think that it is a good thing not to probe the opinion of Copernicus: but this . . . It is important for one's whole life to know whether or not the soul is immortal." [8]

Pascal retreats to the monastery of Port-Royal, wears a hair shirt, and takes part in the theological disputes of his day; he writes brilliantly. Hair shirt and certainty about God and controversy with the Jesuits but also cycloids hold Pascal's attention in his later years; it is said that the methods of calculation he developed were an anticipation of integral calculus. Pascal concentrates on God and cycloids; he carries a scrap of paper in the lining of his coat as a reminder of the night November 23, 1654; he wants to convince his contemporaries of God and the immortality of the soul, and to do it with the help of the calculus of probabilities and the method of calculating with infinite numbers.

Pascal was not destined to publish his thoughts on these matters in book form. His thoughts survived as fragments, and meanwhile Mr. Ogilvy's thoughts have cornered the public-opinion market, Mr. Ogilvy is rich enough to afford a full-page advertisement as a way of getting his ideas across; he is head of a great advertising agency and therefore must have a keen sense of what is or is not marketable. Mr. Ogilvy expresses a widespread view when he says: "It is better to know than to believe." The Enlightenment has won out, and Pascal is remembered as the ancestor of the computer industry. (And, in fact, he did build an adding machine.)

Modern industry pays no heed to the certainties that came to Pascal in the night. The immortality of the soul is the business of philosophers and theologians, who may be allowed to waste a few minutes of our time on certain occasions, even, now and then, at a major meeting of an industrial combine.

Our age's unsatisfied remnant of soul wanders like a ghost through the meetings of businessmen, comes to the surface in hit songs and other popular music (though not in a hair shirt) that asks what does or doesn't come after death. Pascal, the unsatisfied mathematician, anticipates the modern longing for God. In his day, this state of soul was to be found in the Paris salons; today it is universal.

To his interlocutor Pascal suggests a wager in ideas. The wager is not simply a brilliant fancy of a God-seeking mathematician of three hundred years ago, nor does it express a mere notion. It typifies a situation that is universal today. Pascal provides us with an opportunity to make a (somewhat belated) early diagnosis, since all the symptoms that today characterize men collectively were already fully developed in him as an individual. We can learn something from Pascal.

The wager: " 'Either God exists or he does not exist.' But which of the alternatives shall we choose? Reason can determine nothing: there is an infinite chaos that divides us." [9] At the outermost edge of this infinite distance, let us play a game.

The game is the one connected with the calculus of probability: the tossing of a coin. The more often the coin is tossed, the more closely the results approximate to a mathematical law, namely, that the chances are even if the coin is tossed an infinite number of times. In practice, of course, an infinite number of tosses is not possible. Therefore we simply settle the bet: heads or tails?

Pascal suggests such a wager, reasoning with an imaginary skeptic that there are only two possibilities on which to bet: heads or tails, God or nothing.

> If you win, you win everything; if you lose, you lose nothing. . . . In this game you can win eternal life which is eternally happy; you have one chance of winning against a finite number of chances of losing. . . . The uncertainty of winning is proportionate to the certainty of what we risk, depending on the proportion between the chances of gain and loss. . . . And so our argument is of overwhelming force, when the finite

> must be staked in a game in which . . . the infinite is the prize.

The skeptic inquires whether there is any possible way of seeing into the hidden workings of the game. Pascal refers him to the Bible. The skeptic admits he still can't believe: "I am made in such a way that I cannot believe. What do you expect me to do?" Pascal: "Try . . . not to convince yourself by multiplying the proofs of the existence of God, but by diminishing your passions."

The calculus of probabilities and the hair shirt are brought into the wager, as reason endeavors to render plausible what lies beyond the range of reason. The percentage of probability and the differential calculus cannot replace the hair shirt; we are playing for an infinite stakes and must make our bet.

Pascal's thinking oscillates between God and the cycloid; the enlightened skeptic finds pleasure in the arguments of the pious mathematician and places his bet on God and the immortality of the soul. Whether he will also don a hair shirt is left unanswered, as is the outcome of the wager. (Otherwise it would not be a wager.)

The value of Pascal's notion as an example to us does not derive from the reasoning it involves. The men of the Enlightenment lived for two hundred years with a religion of reason, with a God whose existence was rationally established and a soul whose immortality was rationally proved. In their four-dimensional attitudinal space Professors Morris and Bales surely have a place for this kind of mentality; the liberal upper middle class are its (latest) representatives. Pascal's idea is epochal rather because it introduces the notion of a wager into the question of meaning versus absurdity, and because of the uncertainty, curiosity, tension, and readiness to take risks that are thereby brought to bear. Reason proves inadequate to deal with the problem of death and is replaced by a cheerful courageous readiness to stake everything. Let the wager point our way! The entrepreneur needs more than hard work; he must have good luck as well. Anyone who wants to win a bet must cherish the hope that the incalculable may happen; Faust makes a wager with the devil at the beginning of the industrial age.

As long as the industrial age is not yet over, all of us are inspired by the spirit of enterprise, which makes its bets and investments and, no matter how businesslike its calculations, counts on luck as well.

The end result is as undecided as the question of what comes after death. The words that François Rabelais (who wrote *Gargantua* and *Pantagruel*; died 1533) puts on the lips of the dying archbishop of Paris capture a mentality that is widespread today: "I am leaving to look for a great Perhaps." We may cling to this great (or little) Perhaps in all modesty, despite Mr. Ogilvy and Professor Ott.

Anyone looking for a dependable answer to his ultimate questions is politely asked to lay the book aside at this point.

WE SIT IN TEARS

In today's situation, the appropriate way of replying to old Seibold's question may be found in Jean Paul's *Siebenkäs*, where the dead Christ descends from the universe and says there is no God:

> At this moment a tall noble figure with immortal pain written on it descended from on high onto the altar, and all the dead cried out: "Christ! Is there no God?" He answered: "There is no God." The bloodless shadows fluttered away, as the white rime left by a frost melts at the touch of warm breath, and all was emptiness. Then the dead children, who had been roused from their graves, entered the temple, filling men's hearts with terror. They in their turn said: "Jesus! Have we no father?" And he answered with tears streaming down his face: "We are all orphans, you and I alike; we have no father." [10]

Dr. Freud comments:

> They will, it is true, find themselves in a difficult situation. They will have to admit to themselves the full extent of their helplessness and their insignificance in the machinery of the universe; they can no longer be the centre of creation, no longer the object of tender care on the part of a beneficent Providence. They will be in the same position as the child who has left the parental house where he was so warm and comfortable.[11]

Dr. Freud is speaking of men sensibly brought up and not needing the intoxication of religious illusions. He adds: "But surely infantilism is destined to be surmounted. Men cannot remain children forever."

Dr. Freud throws the baby out with the bath; his eye is the tearless eye of the doctor, his diagnosis pitiless. Professor Adorno cannot accept such an attitude:

> In Freud's work, however, the dual hostility towards mind and pleasure, whose common root psycho-analysis has given us the means for discovering, is unintentionally reproduced. The place in *The Future of an Illusion* where, with the worthless wisdom of a hard-boiled old gentleman, he quotes the commercial-traveller's dictum about leaving heaven to the angels and the sparrows, should be set beside the passage in the *Lectures* where he damns in pious horror the perverse practices of pleasure-loving society. Those who feel revulsion for pleasure and paradise are indeed best suited to serve as objects: the empty, mechanized quality observable in so many who have undergone successful analysis is to be entered to the account not only of their illness but also of their cure, which dislocates what it liberates.[12]

We wish to thank Professor Adorno for siding with us against Dr. Freud and justifying the tears we shed for our lost heaven. The dead Jesus opposes the psychoanalysts and speaks to the souls of the children with tears streaming down his face.

We have on hand plenty of buildings, with trained personnel, where such tears could be shed as the collective mourning of our age. The purpose would be to heal the mortal sickness of industrial society and to practice an attitude that would become effective even outside the Churches.

For our next few chapters, then, let us keep Good Friday in mind. The day is marked in the calendar; it has a meaning that is not outdated. Johann Sebastian Bach's *Passion according to St. Matthew* is widely known, and we may think of its final chorus as an invitation to us: "We sit in tears."

After our guided tour through the memory of mankind the participants may be a bit tired. Please sit down; tears are permitted. The dead Jesus preaches from out of the universe to our sick industrial society. He himself cannot help weeping from time to time.

8

No Time for Tears

The fruit and vegetables are always fresh where I do my shopping—a lively market with many stalls. The shopkeepers wrap pickles and mushrooms in old newspapers for their customers, and thus bring the past to life once more. While the mushrooms are steaming over a low flame, the old newspapers have their day again; a glance at the page torn from an old paper can be a source of entertainment as I prepare my meal.

Joe Siffert's death will probably never be fully explained. When the flames of his burning BRM finally died down at Brands Hatch, all that was left was white-hot pieces of metal. Siffert's helmet was still in the car, but his body was burned to a crisp. The BRM team is downhearted and confused. According to Pedro Rodriguez, the British racing team has now lost its second important Formula I driver. Helmut Marko, another BRM driver, who wasn't at Brands Hatch for the start of the meet, has not been in touch with the team since the accident. He learned of Siffert's death only from the television. Marko: "I can't understand it all! Another fellow dead whom I knew so well! It's an especially heavy loss for me because Siffert was behind me in my Formula I ambitions. I'd already known him for a long time from the Porsche team. He was always very helpful and used to give me tips on how to

> drive in a race." Helmut Marko describes his older friend as a tough racing driver, who kept pushing right to the very end of a race. Despite his thirty-five years he was in extraordinarily good condition. Life leaves Marko no time for tears over his friend's death: on Wednesday he flies to Rome; next Monday he opens his own racing show "PS 71" at Salzburg; then he flies to South Africa and will return to Austria only at the end of the year.[1]

Meanwhile my meal is ready. Joe Siffert is still dead, the old newspaper has been thrown out for the last time, life leaves us no time for tears, we can't understand it all. After a meal, the conscientious housewife cleans the dishes and silverware she has used.

Helmut Marko's words in the old newspaper might have come from a professor of philosophy: "I can't understand it all!" (Many philosophers say truth resides only in the totality of things; others maintain totality and untruth go together.) To grasp the truth of Joe Siffert's death Helmut Marko would need time; coming to terms with grief is a lengthy business, according to the psychoanalysts. Mastery of grief requires remembering, repetition, and working things through. But life leaves Helmut Marko no time for tears over his friend's death. Marko has to open his own racing show at Salzburg.[2]

The report of Joe Siffert's death likewise touches the reader only fleetingly. Later, the account serves for wrapping pickles and mushrooms. There are too many newspaper reports, and the reader has the same experience as Helmut Marko: he has no time to come to terms with all the reports.

Reports of racing drivers' deaths are of some interest to readers who are themselves drivers. The old newspaper catered to this interest by its very layout, for the article on Joe Siffert's death had a banner headline: "Only his helmet is left!"

A headline like this immediately triggers in the reader (if he is a driver) a mechanism well known to the experts: Unpleasant news will be more quickly forgotten than pleasant news. Joe Siffert's death has no effect; the new racing show must be opened and there is no time for tears.

The BRM team is downhearted and confused. What happens, or doesn't happen, after death?

"Cut off even in the blossoms of my sins": thus does the ghost of the dead king complain to Prince Hamlet; his violent death prevents him from finding rest.[3] A sudden death for which there has been no preparation is especially fearful, and even among primitive peoples those who died by accident are handled with scrupulous caution. Accidents are a cultural phenomenon unknown in the animal world. A fatal accident or especially a murder is an unpleasant reminder to the survivors of the shadow side of hominization and of the price that must be paid for every cultural achievement. The fishermen's wives wait on the beach to see whether all the men will return home.

From the viewpoint of the history of culture a fatal accident is especially demoralizing. There are several kinds of death. First, there is natural death; no social emancipation has any effect here. Then there is the second death: the bitterness that has pervaded the human condition since the advent of the so-called high cultures; the knowledge of how small a degree of fulfillment the individual can achieve in his lifetime; the feeling of having let opportunities slip; the hunger for justice. Thirdly, and finally, there is violent death: accident or execution or suicide or the soldier's death or death in a crime of violence—always death at the hands of a human being, whether deliberately or by accident. The victim ends up as a statistic (in the suicide rate or the accident count). "One man stands fast, another's killed; one rushes past, another's voice is stilled, DRRumm, BRRumm, DRRumm!" (The end of the story of Franz Biberkopf, in Alfred Döblin's *Berlin Alexanderplatz*, is instructive.)[4]

Violent death creates a mental confusion to the third power: the little girl is victim of a sex crime, the suicide rate in Austria is among the highest in the world. On Sunday, October 24, 1971, the Swiss racer, Joe Siffert, crashed his BRM during the fifteenth lap of the Formula I race at Brands Hatch; seconds later the wreck burst into flames and it was impossible to rescue Siffert.

In Europe an average of seven out of every hundred males born will die in accidents; among females the number is five out of every hundred. Traffic accidents are by far the greatest cause of violent death in most of the industrialized countries.[5]

Joe Siffert is but one of hundreds of thousands who have died in traffic accidents, and the number goes up each year; friend Marko must travel off to the opening of his racing show. Half of all the males who die between the ages of fifteen and twenty-four die in traffic accidents.

In the German Federal Republic nine out of ten drivers wash their own cars.

St. Paul the Apostle can help Helmut Marko and the car-washing drivers to cultivate an appropriate attitude to this kind of death. He gives them a clue in his Letter to the Romans when he writes: "Death came through sin."[6]

The addressees of the Letter to the Romans are long since dead, and St. Paul's statement has become part of the catechism as a decisive proof of the Church's doctrine of original sin. But old Seibold has still not come to grips with what he was told in religion class fifty or sixty years ago. Let us begin from the beginning once again.

The Agni (see chapter 4) have a custom which the ancient Romans also had: before drinking, a person pours out a few drops on the ground. The earth thus gets back a little of what man has taken from it. The action is a kind of gesture of reconciliation: let the earth not hold a grudge because men have dug it up and cultivated it. The same spirit of caution is to be seen at work in many customs current among illiterate hunting tribes. These peoples have a whole set of institutions aimed at reconciliation and appeasement. Before, during, and after the hunt charms are used to persuade the wild animals to understand the needs of man. There are strict regulations to prevent wanton killing of animals; in principle, a hunter's training is geared to protect the environment and shows a concern lest the natural order be excessively disturbed. Consequently, we find among savages a certain nervousness: when they farm, they worry about the possible dangers implicit in their interference with the balance of nature.[7] They are familiar with the principle of enough-and-no-more; it pays to be moderate, the soil is not inexhaustible.

These examples illustrate an attitude that is widespread in mankind. Dr. Freud has given it a name, and reminds us that civilization is largely based on the renunciation of instinct.

Thus, prohibitions of incest control man's erotic impulses, and the (cannibalistic) lust to kill is restrained by sacred laws.

The stricter the prohibition, the stronger the drive it seeks to check.

Evidently, then, there is a force opposing the positive energies at work in hominization. This force is violent and deadly. St. Paul calls it sin.

Violent death inflicted by man is a cultural phenomenon; on this point, Dr. Freud is not to be moved. But despite all the theories on aggression no effective universal cure has yet been found. *Incipit lamentatio Jeremiae prophetae*: Here begins the lament of the prophet Jeremiah.[8]

The collective lament in solemn form may be regarded in this connection as an attempt by mourners to take a good look at the sad condition of man's thoughts and aspirations. There are plenty of occasions for such laments. Jeremiah's occasion, for example, was the destruction of Jerusalem. Another may be the felt need to expiate guilt. But this requires time and a collective act of attention that is hard to come by in an adequate measure, as is evident from the public reaction to automobile accidents. Ralph Nader has had a difficult time of it in the United States.[9] Few people study in the school of Jeremiah the prophet, and Cassandra is not popular with car-washing drivers who have no time for tears. (Unless a father or a brother is killed in an accident, but then the reaction is: "I can't understand it all!").

St. Paul's words in Romans were not intended as an explanation, but rather as a hint and a warning to be vigilant.

The substantive issue, that is, the connection between cultural progress and violence, is as obscure and ominous as the graphs published by the Office of Accident Investigation and Data Analysis. The graphs show a perplexing relationship between industrial production and fatal automobile accidents.[10] If you plot two curves, one for the industrial production indexes and the other for the mortality rate in automobile accidents, the two curves rise and fall in a remarkably parallel way (since 1948). No satisfactory explanation has thus far been found for the increase in fatal automobile accidents in periods of strong industrial growth. Thus an element of the deadliness introduced by sin becomes part of industrial growth. The whole business remains puzzling and inscrutable, but at least we can take a good look at it. We know what reasons we have for weeping. Weeping is better than washing cars; tears wash out the heart.

According to statistics seven percent of the males born into the world will die in accidents, as we pointed out earlier. The newspapers accept the inevitability of the statistics, as may be seen from the formulas they use in reporting accidents: "The road has claimed another victim." So many on the Fourth of July weekend, for example; last year there were more (or fewer). The words chosen are almost religious in their connotations; the idiom follows an ancient model.

Human sacrifice was as widespread among the Greeks, Romans,

and Germans, as among the Phoenicians and Arameans or in ancient Mexico and Japan. We occasionally come across human sacrifices as gestures of appeasement on the part of the high cultures and their technology; we read, for example, of sacrifices connected with building—human beings immured in the pilings of bridges or under a threshold (in the latter case, children were preferred).

Today, young men are the preferred victim in sacrifices to the road (aged fifteen to twenty-four according to the statistics). Most of the victims wash their own cars, so that we might almost call them voluntary victims. At any rate, traffic victims show an energetic disposition: they buy automobiles, tank up on fuel, step on the gas, and are interested in the latest models. None of them want to die in their cars; every driver wants to reach his destination at racing speed, and slow drivers hold up traffic and get cursed at. This energetic, efficient, competitive spirit is in strange contrast to the monotony of the death notices. There are, of course, speed limits and traffic signs and signal lights and tests for drunkenness and the fellowship of the road and traffic planning and the psychology of accidents and seat belts and fog lights and drivers' licenses and traffic reports, but the road continues to claim its victims. What is "traffic," then, really?

We are almost tempted in this connection to raise the question of the relation between individual and society, as sociologists and philosophers are constantly doing. Obviously, the question is always left unanswered; otherwise, why raise it again?

We are thinking (still) of an individual, a statistical individual: twenty years old, single, male, possessor of a driver's license, smoker, shop employee, etc. This individual innocently washes his car on a Saturday and then falls victim to traffic. The traffic continues to flow, made up now of other, no less statistical individuals. From a mathematical point of view, death by automobile aims at a certain quota; at the same time, we must give thought to expanding the network of filling stations.

Or think of a real individual, for example Joe Siffert, who was an outstanding driver. The risks he ran were greater than those of other drivers; it's almost as though the road were a gambling casino, with death on the road having a better chance of claiming a Joe Siffert. (And Helmut Marko, too; he has since given up racing, we are told, because of an eye injury.)

Unfortunately, it has not yet become possible to take the statistical probability of death and apply it in a precise, reliable way to the individual. It is not yet possible to look at a hundred newborn males and pick out the seven who will be traffic victims. Any statistician will tell you the attempt is absurd; statistics serve another purpose altogether.

So the question of the relation between individual and society goes unanswered once again, and the same must unfortunately be said of the relation between the traffic and its victims. One man rushes past, another's voice is still, DRRumm, BRRumm, DRRumm. We can't understand it all, but we go on washing our cars; new oil wells are constantly being dug; the Russians are at work in the Persian Gulf, the Americans in Alaska. Occasionally there are political conflicts over petroleum, along with expropriations and price hikes. Japan takes the lead in building supertankers. The highway over the Brenner Pass (Innsbruck to Bolzano) is a masterpiece of technology that enables vacationing drivers to travel in comfort from Germany to Italy.

We have long since thrown in our lot with the automobile and vacations in Italy, with supertankers and a new automobile every couple of years. In Europe great automobile firms merge, General Motors ranks as an economic world power, Fiat builds cars in the Soviet Union. The economists take the cost in victims into account; we can stand seven victims out of every hundred males.

The question of death to the third power really hits home only to the mourning survivors of a traffic victim; but the question remains no less a purely private one than old Seibold's question. The public quickly and easily forgets its traffic victims; the driving public holds no public ceremonies of mourning for the unknown driver; new automobiles roll from factory to street, and no one thinks of playing taps for every fiftieth car.

The Agni (see chapter 4) believe that almost no death in their country is due to natural causes (such as old age or sickness). They are inclined rather to attribute a death to the cunning of another human being, that is, to some kind of sorcery. Psychoanalysts who observe their behavior speak of this belief as the normal paranoia of the Agni, a kind of collective persecution complex.[11] (When an accused witch makes a fictitious confession and pays a small monetary fine, the case is finished.)

In industrial societies belief in witches has almost disappeared, but in compensation the percentage of those who have really lost their lives through violence is notably higher than among the Agni. What the Agni attribute to witches is taken care of among us by traffic, accidents on the job, and long and extensive wars over a fifty-year period (with the increasing involvement of the civilian population); all this is a matter not of fantasy but of fact. There are, of course, no comparative statistics for the proportion of deaths by violence to all deaths in the developed countries over the last two or three hundred years. But, until the contrary is proved, we may safely claim that the percentage over the long run is far higher than the seven percent given earlier. Death to the third power is a sizable fact in the industrial societies; in common parlance the fact is expressed in economic terms: "Many have paid with their lives; progress exacts its price."

Among the Agni funerals are the ritual of greatest importance. Among us, on the contrary, mourning is becoming an increasingly private affair, with state funerals and tributes to heroes being the exceptions to the rule. This holds for deaths due to human (social) causes as well as for natural deaths. The more modern the manner of the violent death, the more effective is the collective denial of it, as is evident in the case of traffic deaths.

The many victims of progress are dealt with in public in a rather businesslike way and with an impersonal detachment: these people have paid; we are waiting for new customers. Public piety is satisfied by showing the victim's picture in the papers and on television (if he was prominent enough); now and then the widow's picture may also appear. Most of the victims, however, are nameless and appear only as numbers Military monuments do usually carry the names of the fallen. But monuments of this kind are erected and cared for only in small communities; the nation as a whole has to be satisfied with an Unknown Soldier. In villages and small cities the old funeral customs survive, but the big cities must do without them. There is no Tomb of the Unknown Driver.

Nowadays tears are shed only by a few individuals for those who have paid the price; at most there is an occasional conference on the problem of suicide. There is no persistent public attention to death in the third power, no widespread mourning (remembering, repeating, working things through) in order publicly to come to terms with the public violence done the victim; the writer is glad and grateful, in fact, for any reader who has persevered this far. The only thing we have now is the compulsive public recapitulation in monotonous accident reports: "Traffic has claimed another victim"; the network of filling stations must be expanded; this year's auto show promises to be interesting.

The question of what does or doesn't happen after death has already been given a public answer, from a driver's viewpoint, in the case of Joseph Siffert. It followed the standards set by the currently available philosophy; it was short and to the point, and a journalistically striking expression of a normal paranoia: "Only his helmet is left!"

They then went to a place named Gethsemani. "Sit down here while I pray," he said to his disciples.

At the same time he took along with him Peter, James, and John. Then he began to be filled with fear and distress. He said to them, "My heart is filled with sorrow to the point of death. Remain here and stay awake."

He advanced a little and fell to the ground, praying that if it were possible this hour might pass him by. He kept saying, "Abba (*O father*), *you have the power to do all things. Take this cup away from me. But let it be as you would have it, not as I."*

When he returned he found them asleep.[12]

9

Back to the Old Ladies

Madame R. had been employed as a waitress and dishwasher in various restaurants, until she had to stop working at the age of sixty-eight because the job had become too much for her strength. Unfortunately, her various employers had not put her down for old age insurance, and consequently she received only 180 francs every three months, of which 150 went for rent. Madame R. did have some savings that enabled her to hold out for four years. Then a neighbor advised her to see a social worker, who obtained for her a pension of 870 francs every three months, plus 80 francs as a rent subsidy. Since then, Madame R.'s budget has been 8 francs a day.

Each week she consumes three steaks, five pounds of potatoes, some cheese, and a pound of coffee. In the evening she generally eats only an apple with some sugar and butter. On Sundays she dines with a friend who gives her the leftovers to be warmed up on Monday. Regrettably, Madame R. herself has only a small paraffin stove for heating and cooking. For the most part she uses little heat; in winter she stays in bed late, and then spends her days in shops and churches. She often goes to the movies. In Paris there are some movie houses that are cheaper before 1:00 P.M.; there she sits through two or three showings, and then walks home. In general, she does a good deal of walking; she reads the headlines at the newsstands and thus is able to follow the course of world events; her neighbors also give her yesterday's papers.

She is generally satisfied with her life, but housing is a problem. Her rather tiny room in an old upper-class house is on the fifth floor, with the last two half-stories being reached only by steep narrow stairs. The lavatories are hard to get to: half a flight down, then half a flight up, then fifteen steep steps. When Madame R. doesn't feel well, she leans against the wall and looks down the fifteen steps she must descend on her way back and wonders how she'll make it. The neighbors would like to have her room, and she's afraid they may be able to get her put in an old folks' home. She'd rather die than go there, she says.[1] Anyone familiar with the situation in French (English, German, Italian, American, etc.) old folks' homes will understand her feelings.

Wilhelm Seibold writes:

I can say in all humility that I have lived in such a way that I need fear no hell. But where are rest and peace to be found? Hypotheses, however beautiful, are of no help, because they are just hypotheses. Can men on our planet be other than they are? Isn't the claim of every single being in this world a valid one? Why must the animals of our earth live on other animals and vegetation, and we men on animals and vegetation?[2]

Simone de Beauvoir writes:

And that indeed is the very reason why I am writing this book. I mean to break the conspiracy of silence. Marcuse observes that the consumers' society has replaced a troubled by a clear conscience and that it condemns all feelings of guilt. But its peace of mind has to be disturbed. As far as old people are concerned this society is not only guilty but downright criminal. Sheltering behind the myths of expansion and affluence, it treats the old as outcasts. In France, where twelve per cent of the population are over sixty-five and where the proportion of old people is the highest in the world, they are condemned to poverty, decrepitude, wretchedness and despair. In the United States their lot is no happier. To reconcile this barbarous treatment with the humanist morality they profess to follow, the ruling class adopts the convenient plan of refusing to consider them as real people: if their voices were heard, the hearers would be forced to acknowledge that these were human voices. I shall compel my readers to hear them. I shall describe the position that is allotted to the old: I shall tell what in fact happens inside their minds and their hearts.[3]

(Old Seibold writes. Simone de Beauvoir writes. Marcuse writes. I write. This evening, after writing these lines, I shall go down to the church and say Mass for about thirty people, mostly old ladies. They do not write books; they live very much like Madame R. and come to evening Mass in the church every day. Then they go home to their loneliness. Tomorrow I'll go on writing.

The old ladies will very probably not read what I write. These old ladies are mostly people with little education and read no books or few. Besides, books are rather expensive.

Attending Mass is better for old ladies than writing books. There is an incompatibility between my activity as a writer and the situation of the old ladies down in the church; no writing of mine will bridge the gap, and, anyway, some of the old ladies will have died before the book is published. All I can do with my writing is to call attention to the fact that that's the way it is.)

Old Seibold asks questions for which there is no answer in the present state of our knowledge: questions about the cruelty of the nutritional process, questions about redemption. Old Seibold tells me in his letter that he wonders how the world and mankind can be improved. Old Beauvoir is angrier and more energetic than old Seibold (she is about seven years younger than he.) She wants to force her readers to listen to the (human) voice of elderly people.

Old Beauvoir in her book urges her readers to adopt a very specific attitude: "We must stop cheating: the whole meaning of our life is in question in the future that is waiting for us. If we do not know what we are going to be, we cannot know what we are: let us recognize ourselves in this old man or that old woman."[4]

Old Beauvoir is of the opinion that our present-day capitalist society behaves more cruelly to old people than any earlier society did and that this fact is generally passed over in silence, suppressed, or denied. Her analysis could well prove enlightening to old Seibold. She doesn't answer his questions, but she does show why such questions arise in his mind.

The questions of people whose lives have become a burden are as old as the so-called high cultures. Old Seibold (a retired farmer) has a predecessor in the literature of ancient Egypt where, about four thousand years ago, a piece was written called "The Peasant's Lament." Also from Egypt comes the "Soliloquy of a Man Weary of Life." From ancient Mesopotamia we have the "Dialogue of Master and Slave," the "Poem of the Suffering Just Man," and the "Lament of a Babylonian Wise Man over the Injustice of the Gods." The so-called wisdom literature of the ancient East is filled with cries of helplessness, resignation, pessimism, and sadness. A cultivated class, the court clerks, gave vent to their feelings in this way (though nothing changed as a result). The civil servants of the ancient East composed proverbs and formulated questions on the evil in the world and the injustice of the gods, and since then the questions have never been stilled—but neither has a universally accepted answer ever been found. During the winter Madame R. stays in bed late and spends her days in shops and churches. She is glad that she has at least her eight francs a day. She refuses to go into an old folks' home; she'd rather die.

It is not only the elderly over sixty-five who should be invited to public ceremonies of mourning for our sick industrial society. At the age of forty people have already crossed a threshold as far as sickness, loneliness, uselessness, ugliness, weakness, superfluousness, poverty, and bitterness are concerned. We owe Professor Sheppard our gratitude for giving us a scientific presentation of this point as regards the United States; he does it in the framework of a new area in applied sociology called industrial gerontology.[5]

Industrial gerontology deals, on the one hand, with the problems of retirement in the industrial societies, and, on the other, with the problem of those whose age makes it hard for them to find work. Such difficulties begin as early as thirty-five to forty in some branches of industry and become rather severe at forty-five. As an industrial sociologist, Professor Sheppard has been occupied for some time now with the problems of older workers. He is chairman of the research division of the United States Senate's Special Committee on Aging, belongs to the committee of the National Council on Aging, works for the Senate's subcommittee on employment, poverty, and migratory labor, and served in the Kennedy administration's program for the rehabilitation of the cities.

On June 12, 1968, the law against job discrimination on the basis of age went into effect in the United States. It is designed to protect workers between the ages of forty and sixty-five from being disadvantaged in their search for employment solely because of their age.

The economy seems inclined to let workers over forty go and to hire them less frequently than those under forty. In the most advanced industrial society in the world the problem of aging begins at forty. (In Sweden somewhat less than half the population is over forty.)

The young (up to twenty-five) have several traits in common with the old (sixty-five and over): a high rate of unemployment, inner-directed thinking, tendency to depression, difficulty in getting married, and psychic changes taking place.

If it be true that in the industrial societies a person is fully absorbed into the labor force by about twenty-five and begins to be slowly extruded from it after forty, then a tale told by the Grimm Brothers becomes very instructive:[6]

When God had created the world and was determining how long each creature should live, the donkey came and asked how long he was to live. "Thirty years," God told him. The donkey found that too long and pointed out that he did heavy work carrying sacks. So God let him off eighteen of the thirty years. The dog came next and likewise thought his thirty years too long, so God reduced them by twelve. The ape, lastly, did not want to live thirty years either, and got ten taken off. Finally, man appeared, happy, healthy, and lively, and asked God to assign him a length of life. "You will live thirty years," said God. But the man cried: "What a short time! Why, just when I've built my house and gotten a fire going on my own hearth, when I've planted trees and they've had time to blossom and bear fruit, and I'm ready to think of enjoying my life, then I have to die! Lord, give me a longer life!" Gradually the man talked God into giving him the lifespans of the donkey, the dog, and the ape all added together, and that is why he lives for eighty years. The first thirty are his human years and they pass quickly; during them he is healthy and cheerful, is glad to work, and enjoys life. Then come the twelve years of the donkey when one burden after another is laid on his shoulders: he must carry the grain that feeds others, and blows and kicks are the reward for his faithful service. The years of the dog follow, when he lies in the corner, growls, and has no teeth to chew with. When this period is over, the years of the ape mark the end; then man is weak in the head and foolish, does silly things, and is mocked by children.

In the story the difficulties begin at thirty; for the Age Discrimination in Employment Act they begin at forty. The intent of the United States law is to improve bad conditions, whereas the tale is inspired by the sad, ironic realization of the price that must be paid for a long life expectancy.

Between the ages of twenty-five and forty we live in tolerable conditions for the most part; the problems come before twenty-five and after forty when we face unanswerable questions and are aware of the meaninglessness that disappoints all hopes. The young are relatively better off because they still have their human years ahead of them. But at forty they too must ask themselves whether it is all true. Then begins the endless faltering dialogue between masters and slaves with its trivial repetitions, its occasional bursts of rage, and its interim solution of eight francs a day for the Madame R.'s in Paris and elsewhere.

I do not work on any governmental committees, as Professor Sheppard does. I am occupied, among other things, with saying Mass for old ladies. The Mass begins with an admission of guilt, a verbalization of guilt. It is admitted with sadness and is thus kept from being repressed or denied; the admission is for the purpose of remembering it, going over it again, and coming to terms with it in a limited way by means of collective mourning and purifying tears. The confession is not an expression of a dry, despairing, endless remorse, in response to the wish and will of murderers or the god Jupiter, such as we find excellently portrayed in Sartre's *The Flies*. It is meant rather as a tribunal for gentlemen: the gentlemen, old and young, of the high cultures and, more recently, of the industrial societies, who wear good but conservative suits and are called upon to justify their conduct before the old ladies at the beginning of Mass. But these gentlemen unfortunately have no time for such things and instead must attend a conference on the problems of aging in industrialized society. Consequently, I'm left alone in the church with the old ladies; I'm left alone with the victims of progress, and with them I make confession of guilt in the name of others (who have no time for tears).

We begin our First Imaginary General Public Celebration of Mourning for Participants over Forty (though children and young people are heartily welcome) with a text from the sixth century B.C., the Book of Isaiah, chapter 61, verse 7: "Since their shame was double and disgrace and spittle were their portion, they shall have a double inheritance in their land, everlasting joy shall be theirs." [7] It will help to a better understanding of the text if we note that here, for the first time in world history, the twofold shame of the poor as a collectivity becomes a focus of attention (until our own day, however, no one has yet done anything about it).

By "double shame" we may understand here the fact that the poor are not only poor (oppressed, old, etc.)—that is the first shame—but are also stupid enough to crucify their rescuers (the second shame). Here, by the way, I would like to make my own the theological opinion that relatively few people end up in hell. Most people, then, are poor, and because they have been doubly shamed, they will receive a double inheritance and eternal joy. First, they will come to realize their situation, and, second, the spitting will be ended for ever and ever, world without end, always, etc.

What we have here is evidently a pious wish on the Church's part; it doesn't really help the poor. But then, we can't even successfully implement an Age Discrimination in Employment Act; Madame R. will continue to have only eight francs. The only thing the promise of Isaiah does is to create an awareness that undermines the tyranny of the high cultures and, more recently, of the industrial age: an awareness that the poor are indeed subjected to a twofold shame. This awareness already represents a big step forward in rejection of the world we live in or, if you will, in ruthless criticism of the status quo, as compared with the rather widespread indiscriminate acceptance of the status quo by the poor whose (well founded) experience it is that "things rarely improve."

As long as school children must be indoctrinated into the high cultures (no "so-called" before the word, in this instance!), they will not develop a sharp eye for judging what man's aims and aspirations have accomplished—and the text from Isaiah will not be outdated. I have quoted the text because I want to emphasize the great antiquity of the shameful historical situation that forces old Seibold to ask the questions he does and Madame R. to get along on eight francs a day. The situation is no less important a result of man's inventiveness than dentistry is.

We are not telling old Seibold anything new about the experience of life, for he has already said: "I was forced to become a farmer who couldn't get any further education." [8]

What he needs to do now is to see the connection between this "was forced to" and his questions about redemption.

Many people blame Mr. Nixon for the present sad situation; others blame God; still others blame the ruling classes (still the most useful entry in the list of attackable objects).

I am happy to offer my services, if needed, as Mass-priest for the General Public Celebration of Mourning for Sick Industrial Society. As I have already indicated, the first invitation should go to people of both sexes over forty, but children and young people will be heartily welcome.

Since no such celebration has been arranged as yet, I must seek consolation from Donald Duck, among others. Donald Duck is just as imaginary a creation as my General Public Celebration of Mourning, but he is a cheerier being. His entertainment value is considerable, and he sells well. As everyone knows, he was invented by the most popular theologian of our century, Walt Disney (died 1966). We can here only briefly suggest Walt Disney's theological position. While Mickey Mouse successfully carries on a tireless and able campaign against evil, Donald Duck evidently experiences what it is to fail. (See in this connection the teaching of the various existentialist philosophies, especially that of M. Heidegger.) Donald lives in modest circumstances and is constantly in need of money; his rich Uncle Scrooge frequently takes advantage of him and exploits him. (See in this connection the teachings of Marxism.) The theological genius of Walt Disney is to be seen in the fact that despite these rather depressing conditions Donald is able to lead a quite varied and basically happy life. He thus illustrates a very common experience: that our life is too short to wait for equality to be established between rich and poor, high and low.

On the other hand, there is another common and equally real experience that Donald Duck has not had, and the lack of it explains in part why he can console and entertain us: Donald Duck does not grow old.

While Peter was down in the courtyard, one of the servant girls of the high priest came along. When she noticed Peter warming himself, she looked at him more closely and said, "You too were with Jesus of Nazareth."

But he denied it: "I do not know what you are talking about! What are you getting at?" Then he went out into the gateway.

The servant girl, keeping an eye on him, started again to tell the bystanders, "This man is one of them."

Once again he denied it.

A little later the bystanders said to Peter once more, "You are certainly one of them! You are a Galilean, are you not?" He began to curse and to swear, "I do not even know the man you are talking about!"

Just then a second cock-crow was heard and Peter recalled the prediction Jesus had made to him, "Before the cock crows twice you will deny me three times."

He broke down and began to cry.[9]

10

Improving

Et vae tacentibus de te, quoniam loquaces muti sunt: "Woe to them that are silent about you, since even they who speak are dumb."[1]

Aurelius Augustine believes that men must speak of God. Since any speech about God amounts to muteness, silence becomes all the more reprehensible: "Woe to them that are silent about you, since even they who speak are dumb."

This principle can be applied to the people who deal professionally with the sick and dying: doctors and nurses, and the relatives of a patient who has been given up as practically dead. All these people conceal the sick man's situation from him; in modern hospitals the doctor's spate of scientific eloquence gives way to silence once the case has been diagnosed as hopeless. Even the relatives go along unquestioningly with this modern ritual which has no legal basis and yet is observed almost without exception. There is a silent agreement to remain silent in the presence of a patient who is regarded as doomed. According to everything he hears from those around him, the patient is constantly improving until he finally dies.

All available research, as well as everyday experience, shows that modern doctors in the industrial countries prefer to leave their fatally ill patients in ignorance of their true state. An especially penetrating description of this behavior pattern has been given by a group of American sociologists who conducted a six-year study of the ways in which terminal patients are tended in hospitals.

The authors distinguish four main types of situation: the patient has no suspicion and the staff keeps the secret; the patient is suspicious and the staff leaves him unenlightened; the patient is certain of his real condition but he conceals his knowledge and the staff goes along with him; patient and staff alike stop keeping the approaching death a secret.[2]

In the United States an average of about eighty-five percent of the doctors hold that terminal patients should be left ignorant of their condition.[3] In Europe the situation is similar. It can be said that in the vast majority of cases there is no openness between patient, staff, and relatives. All those involved obey a powerful taboo, and in only a few cases is there any complete rejection of secrecy (last of the four phases mentioned above). The taboo is, however, something novel in the history of human culture, for in preindustrial societies there is a much more straightforward attitude to natural death. In the hospitals of Asia you can see the relatives gathering around a dying patient several days before the expected end; the patient knows his condition. In the developed countries, however, the matter is more complex. We quote from a sociologist's interview with a nurse:

INTERVIEWER: Did he talk about his cancer or his dying?

NURSE: Well, no, he never talked about it. I never heard him use the word cancer. . . .

INTERVIEWER: Did he indicate that he knew he was dying?

NURSE: Well, I got that impression, yes. . . . It wasn't really openly, but I think the day that his roommate said he should get up and start walking, I felt that he was a little bit antagonistic. He said what his condition was, that he felt very, very ill at that moment.

INTERVIEWER: He never talked about leaving the hospital?

NURSE: Never.

INTERVIEWER: Did he talk about the future at all?

NURSE: Not a thing. I never heard a word. . . .

INTERVIEWER: You said yesterday that he was more or less isolated, because the nurses felt that he was hostile. But they have dealt with patients like this many times. You said they stayed away from him?

NURSES: Well, I think at the very end. You see, this is what I meant about isolation . . . we don't communicate with them. I didn't, except when I did things for him. I think you expect somebody to respond to, and if they're very ill we don't. . . . I talked it over with my instructor, mentioning things I could possibly have done; for instance, this isolation, I should have communicated with him. . . .

INTERVIEWER: You mean that since you knew he was going to die, and you half suspected that he knew it too, or more than half; do you think that this understanding grew between you in any way?

NURSE: I believe so . . . I think it's kind of hard to say but when I came in the room, even when he was very ill, he'd rather look at me and try to give me a smile, and gave me the impression that he accepted . . . I think this is one reason why I feel I should have communicated with him . . . and this is why I feel he was rather isolated.[4]

Woe to them that are silent about death,
since even when we speak about it we are dumb.

The sociologists:

> Besides the physician's word, what else can the patient depend on if he does want to know his fate? If one were to write a set of directives for such a patient it would go as follows: Apart from making your physician tell you, listen carefully to what the staff says about you. Listen carefully also to anything the medical or nursing personnel may tell you, obliquely, about your condition; for sometimes they flash cues, perhaps unknowingly or unwittingly, about you. . . . By being canny and clever, you can catch them unawares.[5]

The sociologists warn the patient that he has no one who feels obliged to tell him anything:

> Our hospitals are admirably arranged, both by accident and by design, to hide medical information from patients. Records are kept out of reach. Staff is skilled at withholding information. Medical talk about patients generally occurs in far-removed places, and if it occurs nearby it is couched in medical jargon. Staff members are trained to discuss with patients only the surface aspects of their illnesses, and . . . they are accustomed to acting collusively around patients so as not to disclose medical secrets.[6]

Even the relatives keep the secret; even the other patients let nothing slip and are very discreet when death is involved.

Most patients, moreover, have no experience in recognizing the signs of approaching death. They are novices when it comes to dying. They must fight the battle for truth alone; everyone else is an affectionate adversary.

Nowadays more than fifty percent of the patients in the United States die in hospitals. The percentage of those who die at home is decreasing, and not only in the United States.

There is also a tendency to associate dying with hospitals. Relatives are increasingly inclined to make sure that the death takes place in a hospital; there the patient will have competent professional help (and these professionals are experts in keeping silence).

The professional staff (so the sociologists tell us) find dealing with dying patients a heavy psychological burden. Many doctors today specialize in areas of medicine where they do not have to meet dying people. Since most doctors, moreover, prefer to keep the dying patient ignorant of his condition, the main burden of dealing with the dying falls on the nurses. Many nurses admit they prefer working in wards where there are few deaths. When they cannot avoid dealing with the dying, they incline to go about their work in a fatalistic spirit; many can maintain this attitude, others can't. The most common method of dealing with those who (unbeknownst to themselves) are dying is to limit contacts to the necessary minimum. The nurses who do deal with the dying are, however, conscious of their own failure. They feel that they are unprepared to treat the dying and that their training is deficient in this regard. The nurse's obligation to give an account of her work extends only to the technical side of her activity. Whether and about what they speak to the dying is not a matter to be discussed in the routine reports nurses must make.

Modern specialization and modern technology evidently leave their mark on hospital life; this is inevitable. Yet the nurses retain a sad sense of their inadequacy in dealing with the dying, but the feeling bears no fruit and comes into the open only when the sociologists ask their questions. Professional literature (mostly American) on the treatment of the seriously ill and dying is not very extensive. The scientific, technological age is evidently helpless in coming to grips with the final days of a human life. Yet there is no ongoing, public, penetrating, general discussion of this helplessness, because it would undermine the dominant convictions of our age. Our common helplessness is, instead, repressed, forgotten, passed over in silence, as is the lot of the elderly and the statistics on accidents.

The silence of the hospital staff and the silence of the relatives in the face of imminent death is thus only a symptom pointing to a widespread pathological condition that affects contemporary life.

Any words of consolation derived from literature, psychology, philosophy, theology, etc., must be directed only to individuals and make no demands on public opinion as long as the pathological conditions underlying the present state of affairs have not become the object of a widespread critique. Such a critique will obviously be undertaken only when society's illness becomes unbearable to the majority. This is at present not (yet) the case.

The way people die in hospitals is thus a necessary price to be paid for the acceptance in principle of the status quo.

The state of soul of the individuals who have to pay the price is a matter of indifference (again, in principle) to the body of survivors as a whole. The survivors in a given instance may be more or less saddened by the loss suffered, but the collectivity learns no lesson from the inevitable conditions in which the men of our day must die.

When noon came, darkness fell on the whole countryside and lasted until mid-afternoon.

At that time Jesus cried in a loud voice, "Eloi, Eloi, lama sabachtani?" *which means, "My God, my God, why have you forsaken me?"*

A few of the bystanders who heard it remarked, "Listen! He is calling on Elijah!"

Someone ran off, and soaking a sponge in sour wine, stuck it on a reed to try to make him drink. The man said, "Now let's see whether Elijah comes to take him down."

Then Jesus, uttering a loud cry, breathed his last.[7]

11

Better Not to Have Been Born

The annual rate is hardly more than 100 out of every 100,000, or 1 out of every 1,000, at the outside.[1] Relatively few people end their own lives, and yet their action has a strong emotional impact. Even where others respect their decision (as in Japan), we cannot say that these others are indifferent to those who write finis to their own lives. Nowhere is this most logical way of rejecting the world either recommended or desired, although the martyr or hero may become an object of veneration (they are exceptions to the rule). The reaction of people by and large is generally one of abhorrence, fear, and dismay; in German, even the very name for the act is abusive: "self-murder."

In France suicide was a crime until 1790, in Prussia until 1850, and in England until 1961. (As late as 1955, a man who tried to commit suicide in an English prison was sentenced to a further two years of imprisonment; the sentence was appealed and commuted to one month.) Even in the professional literature we can often detect an attitude of revulsion behind the objective tone, as when those who commit suicide are characterized without exception as mentally ill. Suicides form a minority of dissenters from a worldwide belief that has all the authorities on its side: Life is worth living.

In Christianity it was Aurelius Augustine who determined the attitude to suicide as to so much else, and it was, right from the beginning, an attitude of great severity: "He who kills himself is unquestionably a murderer." [2]

The menacing figure that first comes to the Church Father's mind in his polemic against suicide is that of Judas Iscariot with its hint of ineluctable damnation:

> We rightly abhor Judas' action, and the Truth tells us that by hanging himself, far from expiating his crime of treason Judas only aggravated it. For, when he despaired of God's mercy, his deadly remorse cut him off from salutary repentance. With how much more reason, then, should one who has no grounds for punishing himself so severely abstain from suicide!

In Augustine's eyes, even Judas' repentance was impious. The apostle who betrayed Jesus becomes the prototype of all suicides, and the horror of a life gone irremediably astray is evoked in the reader's mind. Suicides are just as much beyond forgiveness as that son of perdition; hell is surely their lot.

The collective sense of horror has shaped the figure of Judas and made a legend of it: there he stands with the cord in his hand instead of the bag of coins he has now thrown away; later on he is turned into a redhead. The stories of Judas in the Bible speak of a field that was paid for with the reward originally given to the traitor and was set aside as a burial place for foreigners. Jerome (died 420) locates this piece of land in the Valley of Hinnom outside Jerusalem. Several biblical ideas evoking terror are given a local habitation and a name by being associated (with the help of what might be called a "geographical method") with the Valley of

Hinnom. (The tourist can look out into the Valley of Hinnom if he walks in the direction of the main railway station. The view from Abu Gate is especially recommended.)

The Valley of Hinnom offers the tourist little worth seeing. Story has it that long ago children were sacrificed there to the god Moloch; that King Josiah later made it a place of infamy by having the bones of the dead burned in it; and that a fire was constantly kept burning there for disposing of refuse. Toward the end of the second century B.C. the Valley of Hinnom appears in contemporary Jewish literature as a place of punishment south of Jerusalem. We are told of a deep dark ravine wherein burns a fire in which apostate Jews are tormented until the final judgment. This idea is anticipated in the last sentence of the Book of Isaiah: "Their worm shall not die, nor their fire be extinguished, and they shall be abhorrent to all mankind."[3]

Around A.D. 50 the Valley of Hinnom (under the name Gehenna) is regarded in rabbinic literature as the place where the damned are punished before the final judgment. The old kingdom of the dead is now identified, though in a vague way, with Gehenna. In any case, Sheol is no longer a primitive land of shadows but a place of punishment and torment. This is true even in the Gospels and even for Jesus: "Better to lose part of your body than to have it all cast into Gehenna."[4]

Jerome, a Father of the Church, later heard the tales current in Jerusalem and found the field in the Valley of Hinnom that had been bought with Judas' blood money. Damnation and the pains of hell took on concrete shape in Judas the suicide. The geography of terror has a place filled with wailing and the gnashing of teeth.

It is understandable that, given such threats, a widespread sympathy for suicides became impossible for a long time. A synod of Arles in 452 maintained that every suicide is (like Judas) possessed by the devil; even today the Roman Church in principle refuses Christian burial to suicides.

The Scotsman David Hume (died 1776) was among the first to take a rational view of the matter in his posthumously published essay *On Suicide.* He claims that the individual has the right to dispose of his own life. Young Werther, who appears on the scene at the same period, makes (literary) use of the right: "There it was at last, solid and unalloyed, the one ultimate thought: I will end my life!"[5]

"I will end my life!" What more penetrating, radical, and total way of rejecting the world (and criticizing society) could there be? Seen from this angle, suicide or attempted suicide is a special case of an attitude—the will to die—which stands in contrast with the usual will to live. Jesus and Judas thus prove to be surprising neighbors; both want to die (even if for different reasons).

Now and then, the will to die seems to lay hold of many at the same time. These are men subject to command: soldiers going off to war, ready to die; usually a goal is set before them, Something Important. But let us not be deceived. The driving force behind the intoxication war produces is not the will to die but the will to slay; one's own death is accepted as a possible result. The important thing is the group that advances together to attack the enemy; as a body that shared the same fate, the group lessens the individual's fear of death.

A clearly expressed will to die usually proves quite disturbing to everyone who hears it. When it is translated into action, it proves highly disconcerting to others (a feeling of confusion, of having lost their bearings, is the first emotion the others experience). Elias Canetti has given one reason for this reaction: "The loss weakens the living and, if it is a man in his prime, is particularly painful for his people. They resist it as well as they can, but they know that their resistance is not much use. The crowd on the other side is larger and stronger than theirs and the dying man is dragged over to it. All their attempts to prevent it are made in full awareness of this superiority."[6]

Rarely do we find on a large scale a sense of ease in the face of the will to die. In the ancient city of Massalia there was a regulation for people who did not want to go on living. They were to make known their wish to the Council of Six Hundred and to give their reasons for it. If the Council agreed, the person received the cup of hemlock. It surprises us that permission to die should be given even to someone who was still living in happy circumstances and simply feared that he might lose fortune's favor; yet even such a person was allowed to end his life.[7]

There are veiled forms of the will to die; no cup of hemlock is drunk, but a man rejects the world in a decisive and radical way. An example of this ascetic attitude is Francisco de Borja, Marquis of Lombay and Fourth Duke of Gandia in Spain, later third General of the Jesuit Order (born 1510, died 1572). His family (Borgia, in Italian) is well known. (The Roman Church venerates him as a saint.)

Francis, then a Spanish grandee, rode in the funeral procession of the dead Empress Isabel of Toledo as it crossed the countryside to Granada and the burial chapel of the Catholic kings. At the tomb, it was his duty, according to ancient custom, to swear to the identity of the dead queen. She had died young, but corruption was well advanced; her features were unidentifiable and Francis could only swear that, given the care exercised in transporting the body, its identity was assured. The retinue quickly disappeared, but Francis stayed on in the crypt, fascinated by the corpse. He spoke to it: "Sacred Majesty, where is the radiant joy that once dwelt in your face? Where your incomparable grace and beauty? Are you really Donna Isabel? Are you really my Empress and Lady?"

Then, the moment of conversion: "What are we about, my soul? What are we looking for? What goals do we pursue? If death can so deal with kings and the great ones of the earth, then what army can stand against him, what power resist him? Would it not be far better to die to the world while we live in it, so that we may live to God when we die?" [8]

Thus, the grandee of twenty-nine; henceforth he does not live with his wife. After her death he becomes a Jesuit to the greater honor and glory of God, renounces his offices and dignities, and is ordained a priest.

The impulse that moved Borgia can be seen at work in history from the Buddha to our own day and has always exercised a strong influence. The thought of death determines how a man will live his life; the instincts, especially the sexual, are put to death while he still lives, so that we may speak of a perduring anticipation of death. The composure which the ascetic thus achieves gives him a great advantage over those who cling to life; death, when it comes, is no surprise to him.

The aging, cancer-stricken Dr. Freud acknowledges: "It is in vain that the old man yearns after the love of woman as he once had it from his mother; the third of the Fates alone, the silent goddess of Death, will take him into her arms." [9]

The dominant theme of Freud's later work was the hypothetical death instinct; according to Freud's theory, the impulse that moved young Borgia is in fact universal, though obscure in its workings.[10] Death becomes the final goal every living thing strives to attain. "On the basis of theoretical considerations, supported by biology, we put forward the hypothesis of the death instinct, the task of which is to lead organic life back into the insensate state." [11]

Job rejected the world when he cursed the day he was born; he would have been better off had his mother miscarried and buried him without ceremony, for then he would be tranquil and at peace.[12]

In times of great suffering men wish they had never been born.

They yearn for their mother's womb: there they had been safe and life was to some extent bearable. Thus lament the oppressed, those—be they neurotics or not—who are cheated by nature (through sickness) or society (through want); many of them draw the logical conclusion. Contemporary research has no sure answer to why it is that relatively few actually put an end to themselves; the suicide (or attempted suicide) rate cannot be explained by any single cause or set of causes. Why is the suicide rate so high in West Berlin (over 40 per 1,000) and so low in Spain (under 10 per 1,000)? We can only guess. Why did this man commit suicide while the next fellow did not, although their circumstances were similar? This is often an unsolvable riddle.

In any event, it is a notable fact that the rejection of the world, which is part of the will to die, is more widespread than suicide. Suicide is, as it were, the ultimate consequence of a certain frame of mind, of which Job is an early example.

The radical rejection of the world, which is Job's response to a life that had become intolerable, is by no means as rare as suicide. Madame R. (for more about her, see chapter 9) would rather die than go into an old folks' home. Her rejection of the world is hypothetical; her will to die is expressed as a possibility because she is not yet in an old folks' home. As I said earlier, it's easy to sympathize with her feelings.

According to Max Weber, rejection of the world has its directions, stages, and forms.[13] Rejection or denial of the world is, in this view, an effective collective effort to create meaning by turning away from reality, which is evil, and thus to attain salvation, or redemption.

In general, the movement is from the exterior to the interior: away from the noise of the marketplace, the partisan struggle, the preoccupation with success, the pleasures of love, and the inquiring rational mind. The historical religions of salvation have existed in constant tension with the world, its ordering of reality, its ways in the economic, political, esthetic, erotic, and intellectual spheres. The great motto has been "All is vanity," a motto adopted first by monks (in India) and later by the masses, on whose lips it became the groan of the oppressed creature. In Weber's view, then, negativity characterizes the religions of salvation and redemption: the rejection of the world, the denial of the world, the unsparing criticism of the status quo—all this at least in germ. In the process, there can be a quick shift from patient resignation to rebellion, as, for example, in the Prisoners' Chorus in the opera *Fidelio* and often in the streets as well (as in Paris, 1789).

When this shift does not occur, or cannot (as in Madame R.'s case), death becomes the secret temptation; the will to die creeps in and waters down the vital urge to continue living, and often with good reason (that is, it is not always the result of a depression generated solely from within). Job leads a procession of thoroughly healthy people; rejection of the world is not something that belongs in the madhouse but is quite justified.

Between justified criticism and self-destructive despair moral boundaries have been drawn, usually in a spirit of bitter anger (as in Augustine), even though the common element of world-rejection is clear in both the criticism and the despair. The view that every suicide must originate in some kind of psychic disturbance springs from moral conviction, not from empirical evidence. The treatment of unsuccessful suicides in the advanced societies is based on that view: the individuals are sent (even against their will) to a psychiatric hospital. It is a fact, of course, that their will to live is often revived in the hospital. Yet the burden of proof is put, a priori, on the patient: it is up to him to prove, in the face of suspicion on the part of the doctors (and the police), that he is mentally healthy.

Those around the person who attempts suicide suddenly become attentive and active. Their indifference turns into busy effort when they are confronted with an unconscious man who is breathing his last; they pump out his stomach. The living do not readily give up one of their number.

It is a known fact that the desire for this kind of attention plays a conscious or unconscious part in many attempted suicides; in these people we find a rejection of the world mingling with the will to live, in proportions that are hard to determine. (The Easter bells ring out, and Faust lowers from his lips the cup filled with the essence of all deadly powers: "The tears well up, and earth possesses me again!")

Suicides are especially distasteful to the hotel business. The Holiday Inn chain has on its staff a full-time chaplain who coordinates the work of a group of voluntary ministers. The latter tend to the 820 Holiday Inns in the United States and have in fact kept 235 guests from committing suicide. In a typical year, a new Holiday Inn is completed somewhere in the world every three days. At present, the Holiday Inns provide 300,000 double beds and put up over 70 million guests a year.

Guests are asked to consult the chaplain before trying to commit suicide.

As it grew dark . . . , Joseph of Arimathea arrived—a distinguished member of the Sanhedrin. He was another who looked forward to the reign of God.

He was bold enough to seek an audience with Pilate and urgently requested the body of Jesus. Pilate was surprised that Jesus should have died so soon. He summoned the centurion and inquired whether Jesus was already dead. Learning from him that he was dead, Pilate released the corpse to Joseph.

Then, having bought a linen shroud, Joseph took him down, wrapped him in the linen, and laid him in a tomb which had been cut out of rock. Finally he rolled a stone across the entrance of the tomb.[14]

12

Cure the Sick

All of us, except for very small children, are survivors. We have buried our dead with more or less solemnity; we have mourned, as best we could; we have wept and realized that there is no medicine against death. (Even God had to die on Good Friday, so we were told in religion class.)

As survivors we know that we ourselves will live on only awhile longer (usually we don't know how long) and that there is no power in heaven or on earth that can keep us from having to die.

Thus far, the facts of Good Friday.

The survivors weep and the tears taste bitter. But after a while the survivors gradually stop weeping; if circumstances are favorable, they get over their loss. The world keeps turning; it's hard to live amid ruins; the survivors reach for their tools: there's work to be done.

On Holy Saturday the surviving apostles begin to ask what's going to happen now. None of them is willing to act as though nothing had happened. Should they simply go on, at least initially, from the point where they were before the catastrophe?

There is certainly plenty to do: "Cure the sick, raise the dead, heal the leprous, expel demons." [1]

The apostles have a clear memory of the Master's bidding, and certainly the task he gave them is by no means finished. There are plenty of sick, leprous, and possessed people, and plenty of dead people, of course. Each of the apostles will be used; no one can be spared. We want to do something, that's why we're here.

Let us now, therefore, speak of dentistry and the successful elimination of the rack and the brave fight against death and the devil—as a first source of encouragement for old Seibold and with our best wishes to a certain lady in Prague whose name we won't mention here (she'd be in trouble with the police if we did).

THE FORCE OF CIRCUMSTANCES

"O yes!" say the Neanderthals, "a juicy bit of flesh really tastes good!" For an awfully long time now we've appreciated a juicy bit of flesh in our mouths; since time beyond reckoning we've enjoyed the flesh of animals. "O yes!" say the Neanderthals, "it's always been true and always will be that we really enjoy the fresh meat of slain animals as we press out the blood and juice with our teeth!"

"It's hard to imagine," say the Neanderthals, "but there are now men who use fire to preserve good fresh meat. We have heard," they say, "that these men even stick tasteless plants into the fire and then eat them."

"It's unbelievable," say the Neanderthals, "that these fellows pick and choose among the eating habits we've observed since time out of mind! Where will we wind up if we start sticking our food in the fire? Fire is for warming yourself and scaring the wild beasts away from the campsite," say the Neanderthals. "Never, never, until now, has fire had anything to do with eating!"

Thus the indignant complaint of the Neanderthals, for, about 40,000 B.C., something new was discovered: cooking. The discoverers were not the Neanderthals but men of the *homo sapiens* type, themselves a recent development. They were inventive people who finally eliminated the Neanderthals and survived with the help of cooking.

The Neanderthals regarded their eating habits as no less

inevitable than sunrise and death. Sunrise, death, the seasonal changes of weather, and other constant conditions of life have all been lumped together under a single name ever since the days of the early Romans; the name is "nature." Anything that has always been so and presumably will always be so we call "natural" in the sense of "self-evident": it's just there, like the solar system, and there's nothing to be done about it. We are also inclined to apply the word "natural" to certain rules of politeness such as the prohibition against murder or the practice of using a knife and fork at table. It's natural and self-evident to us that we must work in order to have food to eat and that children must obey their parents or that persons deserving respect are to be addressed properly or that we should brush our teeth and appear in public only with clothes on.

Are you shocked at seeing our abhorrence of murder put on the same level as the surprise we feel when someone slurps his soup from the dish without using a spoon? But we may safely claim, until the opposite is proved, that there is only a series of gradations between surprise and indignant anger. Recall what was said earlier about opinions, attitudes, and beliefs (chapter 6).

The invention of cooking was as much of a shock to the Neanderthals as the failure of the sun to rise would have been or as the views of Galileo Galilei were to the curial Cardinals. And that brings us to our point, namely, the scientific, technological progress of recent centuries.

The Neanderthals resisted cooking for the same reasons that men a couple of centuries ago resisted the dissection of corpses and are today resisting the worker's claim of autonomy. The master mechanic is at first suspicious of a new method; and indeed it's quite right to resist novelties and stick to tried and true ways, for promising ideas have not infrequently turned out to be foolish.

But the new is not always nonsense, as experience likewise shows—if at least you're ready to admit that pain is unpleasant and to be eliminated if possible. A toothache, for example, can be very unpleasant, but now we have dentistry, and it's more effective than traditional herbal remedies and religious customs.

Obviously, then, there is no standard for deciding in advance whether something new is useful or harmful. There will always be a conflict between inventors and their opponents; the struggle is, unfortunately, necessary and gradually shows us who is right. In the case of the Neanderthals, monarchy, dentistry, and compulsory universal education, the battle has already been decided; the primitives are dying out and traffic is claiming its victims. A decision has been made to apply rational methods in every area; look at the way the electric drill is now being used in dentistry. (Oswald Spengler himself had to visit the dentist occasionally, even though the decline of the West was imminent.)

Persistence in old ways at any price, the Neanderthals' resolute rejection of cooking, the tendency to glorify the status quo, the belief that whatever happens to be is natural and self-evident, and submissiveness to the force of circumstances—this whole complex of attitudes we shall call "prejudice."

We here advise the reader to join the unprejudiced, the inventors, the rebels, in short, all the free spirits (and disciples of Jesus), so as to achieve the right attitude toward death. (Death is still the subject of our reflections.)

In Prague just now the Neanderthals are setting the tone; the lady I mentioned is sad, for she and her friends had other plans, but these are now frustrated. There is a connection between the problems of the lady in Prague and the questions old Seibold is asking; perhaps we can shed some light on the connection.

GOODBYE TO THE MIDDLE AGES

In this context it is important to understand why the Russians burned many churches a few decades ago and have still not rebuilt them. The reaction of peoples living farther west was (and is) abhorrence and indignation. Rarely, however, is it recognized that the vilification of religion in Russia is simply the logical conclusion from ideas and attitudes that had long been coming to the fore in the western countries and have now become quite widely accepted (see Bochum, in chapter 2). Where religion is concerned, the Enlightenment and Communism are simply milder and rougher variants of one and the same attitude, according to which established religion is an obstacle in the struggle against sickness, want, and oppression. Why should it be so regarded? Because religion with its offer of consolation in the next world and its preaching of patient tolerance keeps the faithful from really seeing their wretched condition here on earth and changing it for the better.

These thoughts were given expression over two hundred years ago; they have prevailed as the industrial age has run its course. Today they are characteristic of our time, whether or not they lead to church burning; in other words, they are current both in the Soviet Union and in Sweden.

The World Spirit therefore suggests to old Seibold that he bid farewell to the escapist tendencies of the past which would have him take refuge in the other world. (The old heaven is evidently hard to reconcile with modern dentistry.)

For simplicity's sake, we shall sum up all the things he is to say goodbye to, under the name of "Middle Ages."

These Middle Ages constitute one of the intelligible nuclei of history, according to the principle that

---

> *These intelligible nuclei of history are typical ways of treating natural being, of responding to others and to death.*[2]
>
> Merleau-Ponty

Three such intelligible nuclei have already been discussed in earlier chapters of this book: primitive thinking, the so-called high cultures, and industrial society.

The historical phase that began in ancient Mesopotamia and Egypt and is usually called the high culture phase is what we are here calling, for simplicity's sake, the "Middle Ages." These Middle Ages still survive today, to some extent, in the sheikhdoms of the Near East, but they are disappearing and their decline is instructive.

The Middle Ages brought writing, built cities and irrigation canals, and discovered a division of labor and a distinction of social strata and classes. A further point to be mentioned is that these Middle Ages could only have continued to exist through the use of a force that had men's approval behind it (as we have already pointed out). The Middle Ages of the high cultures has lasted about six thousand years.[3]

The progress of the high cultures during the Middle Ages brought with it a disturbing sense of meaninglessness, to an extent never experienced before. It took time, however, for this sense to make itself felt generally in the heads of men. The first traces of it are to be found in the literature of the ancient East, in the laments of individual wise men at the injustice of the gods and in the rebellious protest of a Job.

At that period, men excogitated a solution that would later become widely accepted. The solution was that the Last Day, the final judgment, and heaven and hell would establish a justice not to be found on earth. First the Jews and later the Christians and the Muslims set their hearts on that ultimate justice.

It took about a thousand years for the idea to become universally accepted; the agency of its spread was what we call the Church. For another thousand years the Church maintained its position in the minds of western men as a typical way of treating natural being and of responding to others and to death. The medieval Church preserved primitive thinking in the form of a belief in souls, reverence for ancestors, and other old customs that were later to be written off as superstition. The new element the Church introduced was redemption and rejection of the world, but this new element was to be found everywhere, even in Buddha and Muhammad and the institutions for the salvation of the masses that these men originated.

Then there arose a fresh new protest against the tyranny of the so-called high cultures. It took the form of a new and penetrating realization of unbearable conditions and a new conviction that brought the best minds into the likewise new laboratories and banks of the capitalist era and into leadership in the workingmen's movements. Those who stayed behind in the Churches began to look more and more like sectarians; they shut themselves off, became touchy and bitter, constantly went in for new reforms, and yet could not escape the stigma of decadence.

In Russia the Middle Ages received short shrift. Elsewhere the process has been long drawn out and is called secularization. But the direction events are taking is everywhere evident, even if with differing degrees of clarity.

The presupposition, then, for any further discussion is that we have a past, in fact a double past: one primitive, the other medieval. This past perdures; not all the churches have been burned down. To turn to the present (on Holy Saturday) means, therefore, to bid a polite farewell to all that is dead and buried and, as such, definitively past and over with. It means to say goodbye to the dead waters (Aigues-Mortes) and the cuneiform tablets, and to the endless cemetery that is preserved for tourists and museum keepers and professors and curators of monuments—a polite and admiring goodbye that pays attention to the stars in the guidebook. (Two stars invite you to make a sidetrip; one star means the thing is of some interest.)

There are people who simply cannot turn energetically back to the present after the period of mourning is over. They keep the dead person's room just as it was, down to the last detail; they live in the past and neglect the present and future.

Holy Saturday offers us quite a different solution: "I must work while the day lasts; the night is coming, when no man can work." [4]

HOPELESS BUT NOT SERIOUS

In the biblical Apocalypse, an eagle flies high across the heavens and cries out in a loud voice: "Woe, woe, and again woe to the inhabitants of the earth from the trumpet blasts the other three angels are about to blow!" [5] (Four angels have already blown their trumpets, and the consequences have been very unpleasant: hail, blood, and fire fall from heaven, a flaming mountain is cast into the sea, a star named "Wormwood" falls from the sky, etc.)

Terror when confronted with expected catastrophe need not always be so great. We are told that the German staff officers in the First World War said that the situation was serious but not hopeless. The Austrian officers, however, turned the words around: "This situation is hopeless but not serious."

The Executive Committee of the Club of Rome tends to talk like the eagle of the Apocalypse:

> Even if the consequences anticipated by the model were, through human inertia and political difficulties, allowed to occur, they would no doubt first appear in a series of local crises and disasters.
>
> But it is probably no less true that these crises would have repercussions worldwide and that many nations and peoples, by taking hasty remedial action or retreating into isolationism and attempting self-sufficiency, would but aggravate the conditions operating in the system as a whole. The interdependence of the various components of the world system would make such measures futile in the end. War, pestilence, a new materials starvation of industrial economies, or a generalized economic decay would lead to contagious social disintegration.[6]

The Club of Rome is an informal committee of about seventy scientists of very varied leanings, from twenty-five countries. It was set up in 1968 as a source of information for political decision-makers as they try to cope with the worldwide problems of mankind. The Club of Rome commissioned a study on the future of mankind which was carried out at the Massachusetts Institute of Technology by an international team of scholars, and published in 1972.

The conclusions the Report reaches are so depressing that the Executive Committee, in the critical evaluation it appends to the book, uses almost the identical words attributed to the German staff officers: "In any event, our future is one of very grave concern, but not of despair."[7] The committee also speaks of a spiritual change of Copernican proportions as necessary if there is to be a basic shift in the values maintained and the goals sought by individuals, nations, and the world community as a whole. As we can see, old Seibold is not the only one asking questions; perhaps he should be made a member of the Club of Rome.

The Committee finds itself forced to admit that, despite the help of computers, we are working under a regrettable handicap: "Although all major world issues are fundamentally linked, no method has yet been discovered to tackle the whole effectively."[8]

Old Seibold is under the same handicap (and has no computer to help him). We must be modest, then, in our hopes of gaining a theoretical mastery of the world's problems.

In addition to its call for what in biblical terms amounts to a conversion, the Committee expressly requires a readiness to make personal sacrifices. (Indeed the Committee sounds like the Pope preaching.) If science can adopt this tone, then the situation is evidently serious (but not hopeless).

The whole problem is how to convince men generally, especially in the highly developed countries, that the situation is indeed serious. People in these countries go on reading Donald Duck and books about the alarming future of mankind; they go out to the movies and then to dinner: the situation is hopeless but not serious.

SPEECH IN SALZBURG

Old Ernst Bloch came to Salzburg for a Conference on the Future of Religion, held at Schloss Klessheim in September, 1970. Famous intellectuals from around the world, and a public interested in hearing them, gathered there for a few days. I accepted my own flattering invitation to attend and, being invited also to take part in the discussion, I did what I thought right: I kept my mouth shut for the most part. When old Ernst Bloch speaks, everyone else should, in my opinion, keep his mouth shut for the most part and listen. After his speech, there really wasn't much left to say, but most of the participants didn't seem to realize this.

Because old Bloch's eyes were weak and he couldn't read any more, he gave his speech extempore; his face with its sharp beak reminded me of a bird of prey. His speech had something that was otherwise almost completely missing from this Conference on the Future of Religion: I mean seriousness. His theme fitted in with the busy inconsequentiality of the other addresses like a fist in the eye, for he spoke of belief in the devil and of the evil in the world. (Professor Toynbee did not come; his keynote address was available to the participants only in writing.) Here I would like to thank old Bloch for coming to Salzburg and giving his speech; except for him and his speech I might just as well have saved myself the journey to Salzburg.

Old Bloch, then, spoke very tellingly about a subject on which usually only researchers interested in aggression speak and write. He asked questions which are important and unanswered, as he sat there with his sharp beak and earnest manner, a simple, disconcerting, and courageous man. (I recommend the reading of his speech.)[9]

Here are some of the things old Bloch said:

Presupposition: The world around us doesn't look very human, nor does freedom seem to reign.

Example: There are countless unintelligible happenings such as the one at Auschwitz when a bored SS officer had some gypsy and Jewish children brought to him, seized them by the feet and kept beating their heads against the wall until their skulls were smashed and their brains dashed out; then he threw the corpses away, washed the blood from his hands, and, because he did not know what else to do, wrote a letter to his wife in which he inquired about his children, who were the same age as, and looked very much like, the children he had just slung against the wall. (Clarification: Auschwitz is past, yet it is still with us; only the victims have changed. Today we have the goings-on in Vietnam and Brazil and so many other places. No matter where we turn on the national and international scene, things look pretty much the same; for the most part we can only stand confused and troubled before these strange and horrifying events.)

Thesis: Evil is still with us!

Findings: Because we have failed to struggle against the demonic as an entity or, better, a being, an essence, we are disconcerted as we look at a world in which such things can happen—and not only among us men, but in the world at large: a world familiar with cancer as well as with Auschwitz, cancer and the appalling indifference of the cosmos to us. The cosmos is not even opposed to us; it is simply alien and has nothing to do with us. The moon in its entirety is like the side it shows us: dead and empty. In other words, we and the cosmos have nothing in common. That, too, is an uncanny fact which we can't even conceptualize—though, of course, we do have a catchword to take care of it: we talk of nature being humanized (Karl Marx himself said that!).

Questions: How fascism and Stalinism come into existence are further questions that belong here, being additional evidence of the noteworthy fact that things which begin well later become suspect; they do not preserve their original purity but deteriorate. The Sermon on the Mount produced the Donation of Constantine; Leninism produced Stalinism; the citizen turned into the bourgeois. Everywhere the worm is at work. But we do not know yet what it is, apart from the intrigues of the ruling classes, that so often causes the corruption of what is best.

Concluding judgment: We must take great care that through the work of our hands and the concepts that light our way, the possibilities before us (a sea of possibilities infinitely larger than the sea of the now given) will lead to happiness and salvation, and not to disaster.

RELIGIOUS INSTRUCTION (CONTINUED)

In today's class, dear children, we want to reflect once again on the reason why you must always sit so quietly in church. Dear children, you know you should not chatter in church or chew gum or laugh or play hide-and-seek in the confessionals. You have often told me that you find it boring in church and that you're glad when you can escape and get outside. You must realize, dear children, that your parents and instructors and superiors and catechism teachers have put a great deal of effort into getting you to sit still, for there's no denying you have a strong tendency to move about and shift around, as well as to be lazy and late for things. You also know, dear children, that grown-ups may not by any means leave off their efforts and that you are still tempted to move around sometimes at your place in church or to chatter a bit. In the same way, it is difficult and takes a great deal of effort to train you not to be constantly getting your clothes filthy and to put on a sweater when it's cold outside and to do your homework and think of the future.

You remember, perhaps, dear children, that Jesus said to the grown-ups: "Unless you change and become like little children, you will not enter the kingdom of God." [10]

You can imagine, dear children, what confusion it would cause if grown-ups took these words literally and how beautiful and exciting and varied and creative this confusion would be! But grown-ups have preferred not to heed the advice and have taken the precaution of locking up this unruly Jesus in the Church. Instead, you have regular meals, and, when you grow up, you too will have children and provide them with regular meals. You will forget that you were once young and had no love for an ordered life; then you will love the ordered life and will teach your children a love of order. You won't be quite sure why people must eat at regular times and not just when they are hungry. You won't be quite sure why disorder troubles you, but you will be happy and satisfied and perform your military service and occasionally drink a bit more than you should, just as your papa now does. Your papa, too, has done his military service, but he can also drink a bit more than he should from time to time. Perhaps your papa finds things boring now and then, and so he has to drink a bit more than he should.

You should not resent your papa, dear children, when he occasionally drinks a bit more than he should. You must realize that your papa finds love of order a strain; so it is understandable that your papa should now and then drink a bit more than he can carry and even that your papa often hits your mama when he's had a bit more to drink than he should and flies into a rage.

If you find it disagreeable, dear children, that your papa occasionally drinks too much wine and often doesn't even come home but perhaps spends the night with a strange woman you don't know, then you must begin to reflect seriously. If you have begun to reflect seriously and are determined not to stop reflecting too quickly, then you'll run into some cold hard facts, lying there like crocodiles that don't stir and yet are very voracious. It's because of them that you must sit still in church.

You will have noticed, dear children, that Punch often gets into a fight with the crocodile and keeps hitting the crocodile until the crocodile is killed. You will also have noticed that the next time the Punch and Judy show comes around, the crocodile is there again, even though he was killed in the earlier show. You see, therefore, dear children, that you can't kill the crocodile as easily as you'd like.

Be cunning and on the watch, dear children. The crocodile is not always easy to recognize, for he takes on various shapes and has many helpers. Strike hard when you run into him; be patient when you strike, but strike hard!

SANE MADMEN

At the present time we cannot give a satisfactory theoretical explanation of the connection between the problems of the lady in Prague and the questions old Seibold is asking; we will take old Bloch's word for this. Death and the devil go together like raising the dead and expelling devils. The apostles decide simply to go ahead with their work, for there is no General Theory of Evil.[11]

But in any case we do need light for our path (more on this later), and we also need a diagnostic tool, that is, the kind of knowledge we can apply to ourselves and others in an effort either to cure ills or to stand up for certain values. A little more concretely: the point at issue is the choice we must make with regard to the definite, deliberate revulsion we feel in certain instances. Here we must return to Professor Bales's UNF type (chapter 6), but not in the purely pragmatic spirit that marks the Professor's handling of the matter.

At this point it becomes necessary to refer back, for the first time, to what I said in the opening chapter of this book.

I had certain experiences with violin playing and cameras and sexual love (entirely forbidden); in connection with these matters I became acquainted with certain people; I learned to regard these people as dangerous (even though I tried, and still do, to deal courteously with them). In my early days I submitted to these people and tried to imitate them; now I no longer want to be like them and I seek my friends elsewhere.

The story of how a keen eye for UNF was developed began about forty years ago in Germany (Frankfurt am Main), led to the United States, and has ended (temporarily) in Prague. Jews play an important part in the story as agents of enlightenment, and the story is thus in fact really a very old one, since the experiences on which it is based are as ancient as certain parts of the Bible. (But, note well, only certain parts of the Bible.) It is a story of books written by men who had no voice in world politics—which is one reason why world politics has turned out the way it has, and not otherwise. It is also a reason why UNF should be so important in world politics, and not Theodor W. Adorno, whom we have already mentioned several times. Our story starts with him.

In 1930 Adorno became professor of philosophy and associate of the Institute for Social Research at Frankfurt am Main; Max Horkheimer was its director. The two friends were interested in fascism and National Socialism; their interest was, however, a highly critical one, and the two had to emigrate to America when Adolf Hitler (1889–1945) became Chancellor of the Realm. Horkheimer finally landed at Columbia University in New York and was able to keep his Institute going there. In 1938 Adorno joined Horkheimer in America.

Adorno's years in America produced, among other things, a book that has had an important influence on empirical social research. It dealt with fascism and appeared in 1950 under the title, *The Authoritarian Personality.*[12] It offers a scale for measuring certain dangerous attitudes; the scale is called the F scale (F for fascism).

Thus, the F in UNF comes from Theodor W. Adorno and his co-workers in the United States, where further empirical research of a very precise kind was done on fascism and prejudice and authoritarianism. (Adorno and Horkheimer had meanwhile returned to Frankfurt.) Among the many works published since 1950 on the subject Adorno had initiated we may single out Professor Rokeach's *The Open and Closed Mind* (1960).[13] Rokeach provided, among other things, a scale for studying dogmatism. He found a connection between authoritarian Communists (and Catholics) and dogmatism. Professor Rokeach thus concentrated his scientific attention on narrowmindedness as manifested in authoritarianism and dogmatism and prejudice and intolerance and fascism and piety and fidelity to conviction, whether on the left or on the right; his work was being done fifteen years after the death of Hitler and seven years after the death of Iosef Vissarionovich Dzhugaskvili (also known as Stalin).

In 1968 the Russians invaded Prague.

In 1969, Horkheimer and Adorno wrote: "In a period of political division into enormous power-blocks, objectively set on collision, the sinister trend continues. . . . Today critical thought (which does not abandon its commitment even in the face of progress) demands support for the residues of freedom." [14]

Adorno died in 1970. In the same year Professor Bales published his book, *Personality and Interpersonal Behavior* (source of the UNF formula); old Bloch and old Horkheimer exchanged greetings in Salzburg at the Conference on the Future of Religion. The lady in Prague was doing household work.

We may now take a critical look at UNF, using three questions which Professor Bales has come up with as a means of picking out certain ways in which men relate to their fellows. The questions are as follows:

> Is it your impression that the person making the statement wants to be in a dominant position in the group? If *yes,* then = U.
>
> Do you feel that the person making the statement likes most people in the group? If *no,* then = N.
>
> Do you feel that the person making the statement feels himself to be allied with conventional legitimate authority? If *yes,* then = F.[15]

(Mnemonic for children, as a supplement to their most recent religious instruction: "Twice yes and once no—The crocodile is on the go.")

We may now summarize Professor Bales's discussion of the personality traits that make up the UNF type. UNF probably shows a high degree of intense prejudice. The F scale constructed by the authors of *The Authoritarian Personality* is usually interpreted as applying to this kind of person. In fact, however, UNF is more likely to express than to agree with the value judgments of the F scale. A careful use of the F scale as a questionnaire would bring to light rather the PF type. "It is an ironic and important fact, if indeed true, that the proponent of autocratic authority [UNF] and the proponent of altruistic love [PF] tend to cooperate in this way." [16] UNF is inclined, moreover, to be thick-skinned, assertive, and adventurous, as well as neurotic, psychopathic, and manic. He is moderately high in suspiciousness and jealousy, and in the inclination to what is called feminine masochism. On the other hand, UNF is low on ego-strength, trustfulness, and accessibility.

For the most part UNF goes his way unhindered, belongs to the editorial staff of newspapers or the organizational staff of political parties, occasionally becomes a bishop or a bank president, delivers speeches or writes letters to the editor. When UNF has a say in things, the tanks roll, young men must cut off their long hair, refractory poets and intellectuals get locked up. UNF advocates tranquillity and order and energetic measures against rabble of all kinds. UNF regards national honor as very important and dislikes the Jews; in his book, the Jews are atheists and seditious elements to whom nothing is sacred.

No research has thus far been done to determine how necessary the support of UNF people was to Adolf Hitler in his seizure of power in 1933, or how great the readiness to obey the UNF type must be in a given population for successful UNF coups or elections or wars.

In fact, entirely too little study has been devoted to the UNF type.

For this reason, UNF beliefs are often regarded as healthy or even natural and self-evident.

In the light of these remarks there can be no further doubt that, as far as the subject matter of this book is concerned, UNF must be regarded as a sane madman.

Why? UNF is a killer, with a strong bent toward death (of

others), and would really like to be the last survivor of a carnage. (UNF is well fitted to be a member of the secret police or a torturer.)

These conclusions go a bit beyond the empirical scientific evidence. To justify them, we must appeal to Elias Canetti and Dr. Freud, both of whom see a connection between love of order, intense anger, and preoccupation with death. Or we may recall the statement of General Stumm in Robert Musil's *The Man Without Qualities*: "Order somehow creates a demand for bloodshed."[17]

The hardest thing to acknowledge, however, is that I too am UNF.

13

Fish Stew and Religious Fervor

Lent was rather monotonous, without a single long weekend (though we did go skiing). At Easter, however, if you're shrewd, you can get in a week's vacation and travel to Spain (for example). (The tourist making ready for a trip hesitates between the many and varied possibilities and helps himself make up his mind by reading articles on travel in the newspaper.)

I quote from an article on travel that gives a good insight into modern man's state of mind and also attracts us to Barcelona.

> Perhaps you'll want to get acquainted with the outstanding dishes to be had in Barceloneta, the fishermen's quarter; if at all possible, one of these dishes should be a hearty *zarzuela*, a fish stew with the reputation of being better even than the bouillabaisse of Marseilles. Then, after crossing the Gothic Quarter, you should visit the cathedral, a place of deeply moving religious fervor; its melancholy will seem doubly expressive in the dusk of dying day.[1]

Old Seibold has been doing a lot of running around: I've taken him to Salzburg and Zürich, the Valley of Hinnom and Aigues-

Mortes, Millstatt and Kirchberg and Paris. Why shouldn't he spend Holy Saturday evening in Barcelona over a hearty *zarzuela* and amid the moving religious fervor of the cathedral in the Gothic Quarter? Perhaps both will be a source of strength. At any rate, I'll do my best.

COMFORT YE MY PEOPLE

The oratorio *The Messiah* by G. F. Handel (died 1759) is, in the words of H. Kralik, "one of those masterpieces that scale the highest reaches of the human spirit."[2] The Overture is directly followed by a recitative: "The violins spin out a lovely larghetto that brings consolation and peace to heart and spirit; the voices repeatedly alternate with this blissful melody and spread their balm."[3]

The text of the recitative (written in E major) is taken from the Book of the Prophet Isaiah, chapter 40, verses 1–3. (Chapters 40–55 of this Book were composed in the sixth century B.C., much later than chapters 1–40, and are therefore known as "Second Isaiah.") The verses appeal to the prophet to comfort his people and tell them their enslavement is at an end.

Dr. Freud is not minded to heed the appeal: "Thus I have not the courage to rise up before my fellow-men as a prophet, and I bow to their reproach that I can offer them no consolation: for at bottom that is what they are all demanding—the wildest revolutionaries no less passionately than the most virtuous believers."[4]

Dr. Freud speaks of an eternal struggle between love and the death urge, that is, between the life instinct and the destructive instinct. He remarks: "And it is this battle of the giants that our nurse-maids are trying to appease with their lullaby about Heaven."[5]

Now the words of consolation in Second Isaiah are, in the original text, not a lullaby at all but a reference to a real opportunity of ending the Babylonian exile and returning to Jerusalem. The hope was fulfilled, under Cyrus, beginning in 538 B.C. (and again beginning in A.D. 1948).

Can Holy Saturday evening (with fish stew for tourists, and the Gothic religious fervor that goes with it) offer nowadays only a cheap religious consolation along the lines of Dr. Freud's appeasing lullaby? We can decide by applying the criterion of the real opportunity Second Isaiah speaks of; we need not appeal to any sense of bliss and balm in the concert hall.

In other words, we can make an estimate of what, for example, a contemporary tourist spending Easter in Barcelona may expect as he walks through the medieval quarter toward the cathedral after enjoying his industrial-age fish stew. (Without the advances of the scientific, technological age he'd not be able to play the tourist and have his stew.) The modern tourist may expect medieval religious fervor to provide him with a real opportunity in the struggle of the two giants Dr. Freud talks about. If he doesn't get it, he can move straight on to the Plaza Real where there's a cafe with outstanding flamenco dancers.

WHAT DO I NEED TO DO FURTHER?

The newspaper article we quoted speaks of "religious fervor," "deeply moving," and "melancholy," not of "bygone beauty," "artistic," and "harmony." Obviously, the article could have used these latter catchwords, too; people often do when discussing Gothic cathedrals. Yet it is no accident that travel articles occasionally cultivate melancholy and dusk (of dying day) when describing medieval cathedrals. For, the industrial tourist wants something else after his fish stew beside bygone beauty. He may even want something radically different but be unable to put a name on it, like the rich young man in the Gospel who can only express his feelings negatively: "What do I need to do further?"

> As he was setting out on a journey, a man came running up, knelt down before him and asked:
>
> "Good Teacher, what must I do to share in everlasting life?"
>
> Jesus answered: "Why do you call me good? No one is good but God alone. You know the commandments: 'You shall not kill; you shall not commit adultery; you shall not steal; you shall not bear false witness; you shall not defraud; honor your father and your mother.' "
>
> He answered: "Teacher, I have kept all these since my childhood. What do I need to do further?"
>
> Then Jesus looked at him with love and told him: "There is one thing more you must do. Go and sell what you have and give to the poor; you will then have treasure in heaven. After that, come and follow me." [6]

Two points in this story are worth noting. The first is the young man's wish. As wish and impulse his desire is thoroughly real; it is neither opium nor illusion (as Marx and Freud respectively use these words).

The second is the Master's answer. It sets a practical condition for everything that may follow; it is not theoretical but a stimulus to action, and it hits the target dead center: "At these words the man's face fell. He went away sad, for he had many possessions." [7]

Two points are also to be noted about our tourist's visit to the medieval cathedral in the dusk of dying day (after his fish stew): the first is the wish he may feel for what he still lacks, for the goal never reached and the task never finished, and the second is that, as we expect from a tourist, his wish does not lead to action.

For, usually the tourist is not changed by his visit to the cathedral; he strolls around and leaves, and ends up perhaps at the Plaza Real and the flamenco dancing.

(Now as in the past, two-thirds of mankind cannot be tourists and enjoy fish stew or flamenco dancing. They are the poor. The young man goes away sad.)

Old Seibold and people like him find themselves unable to help the poor in an effective way—because they themselves are poor or politically powerless or simply weary for the moment from working for a better future. For the sake of this sector of the population (not, therefore, for UNF people and bored murderers) we shall look a little more closely at the inclination of the industrial-age tourist to visit Gothic cathedrals in the dusk of dying day with a view to eternal life.

> *It is a fact worth noting that the decline of religion almost coincides with the beginning of the social revolutions and the growing desire for a better kind of life. In my opinion, when the dogmas of resurrection from the dead, last judgment, and eternal life are rejected, man's need of endless happiness becomes fully evident and stands out in sharp contrast to the wretched conditions of his life on earth.*[8]
>
> Horkheimer

(Orthodox psychoanalysts, disciples of Billy Graham, hard-line Marxists, and curial Cardinals, as well as Mr. Ogilvy, are asked to read the above passage twice.)

For our younger contemporaries (old Horkheimer may be too ancient for them) we add another quotation that fits in nicely here. It is from P. Handke and expresses a man's feelings as he visits a church:

Religion had long been repellent to me, yet I longed to relate

> to something. It was unbearable to be alone and isolated. It must be possible for two human beings to belong to each other, to establish a relationship that is not personal, fortuitous, and ephemeral, not based on a fraudulent and continually extorted love, but on a necessary, impersonal bond. Why had I never managed to be as unreflectingly loving to Judith as I was now while looking at this church dome or at the drops of wax on the stone floor? It was ghastly to have such feelings and not be able to get out of myself! To stand there in dull-witted piety, wholly immersed in objects and movements.[9]

The feelings of the industrial-age tourist in a cathedral are aptly expressed here. Not a very consoling picture, you say? But a bird in the hand is worth two in the bush.

RELIGIOUS INSTRUCTION (CONTINUED)

Cathedrals obscurely remind tourists of Jesus Christ. Somewhere in a cathedral there will always be a hanging or standing cross that reminds the tourist for a moment of Jesus' death. The question arises in his mind: What was so special about this death? How is this death to be interpreted? He turns to the professors for information.

Luckily, we have at hand a dissertation accepted by the Catholic Theological Faculty at Münster in 1969 and published a year later. It deals solely with the theological significance of Jesus' death.[10] The author sums up as follows:

> Jesus did not move unsuspecting toward his death. He had taken into account the possibility and, very likely (toward the end), the certainty of a violent death.—Nothing permits us to say that Jesus directly willed this violent death.—We do not know for sure whether Jesus saw a special significance in his death or, if he did, what that significance was.—It is

> improbable that Jesus attached the ideas of sacrifice and expiation to his death and that he intended to redeem the world by his death.[11]

Christians in the early centuries elaborated various interpretations of Jesus' death. Among them were these:[12]

First: The violent end Jesus met was the usual fate of prophets. The important thing is that Jesus will be returning very soon for the final judgment.

Second: The death of Jesus was willed by God and foretold in the sacred books of the Jews.

Third: The death of Jesus was in expiation for the sins of the past.

Fourth: With Jesus the old order passes, and the kingdom of freedom and love is inaugurated (thus St. Paul).

In the Middle Ages, the following interpretation was worked out. By his sin man upsets the divinely willed order of the world. As a finite being he could not, however, offer the satisfaction due to an infinite God. Consequently, a God-man must freely go to his death; Jesus was this God-man, and that is what he did. The result: God's honor was restored. (Thus said Anselm of Canterbury, died 1109.)[13]

These, very briefly, are the most important interpretations of the death of Jesus according to the dissertation we mentioned. (Thomas Aquinas is omitted here for lack of space.)

Dr. Freud's comment on all such interpretations is that a community no less than an individual develops a superego and that the superego of a culture "is based on the impression left behind by the personalities of great leaders." [14] He observes that

> during their lifetime these figures were—often enough, even if not always—mocked and maltreated by others and even dispatched in a cruel fashion. . . . The most arresting example of this fateful conjunction is to be seen in the figure of Jesus Christ—if, indeed, that figure is not part of mythology.[15]

I have never forgotten the thirteen-year-olds to whom I taught religion almost twenty years ago and who are now grown-up tourists. They chattered away during religion class and sat bored while I told them of Jesus. They were the children of workers or of the lower middle class, and in their own fashion they indulged in a critique of religion (without ever having read Marx or Freud). I think of them when I attend intellectual affairs like the panel discussion on the Future of Religion (at Salzburg; see above), because from them I learned a lesson about religious instruction. I'd like to thank them now, belatedly, for it.

Any revitalization (not just for old Seibold) to be derived from a visit to medieval cathedrals must be judged by strict standards. And I'm referring not just to the standards of Dr. Freud and Karl Marx and old Horkheimer and young Handke with all their books, but to the standards of my former pupils. We should be aware of what those former pupils now yearn for; perhaps they themselves don't know or can't express it. We hope, though, that they do have a sense of something missing; we hope so.

INSIDE THE CATHEDRALS

What Dr. Freud tells us of the disdain on his son's face as he listened to religious stories (see chapter 2) is confirmed by the behavior of my former pupils.

The personnel of the various cathedrals, churches, and chapels are well acquainted with that look of disdain, and they get their backs up at tourists and their disrespectful attitudes. In the churches much visited by tourists the authorities post signs in many languages reminding visitors of regulations to be observed in the house of God. Tourists are asked to wear suitable dress and not to walk around or take pictures during the services. Loud laughter and talk are out of place and to be avoided.

So then, among the at least one hundred million Christian tourists of the West, the personnel of the medieval cathedrals have observed a certain lack of respect in regard to traditionally accepted behavior. It is evident that the tourists have little intention of praying when they visit the cathedrals; they carry guidebooks, not prayer books.

The authorities reluctantly let the tourists have the cathedrals during the day. The authorities believe cathedrals are for prayer, but, as we have seen, the tourists do not share their view. To the tourist, religious fervor is something you gaze at, not something you practice.

On the other hand, tourists do not object to the personnel trying to preserve religious fervor. If the cathedrals were turned into museums, the tourists would be distressed; they have no desire to carry their lack of respect or their disdain for religious stories that far.

During the tourist season a silent struggle goes on in the cathedrals between faithful and tourists. Morning and evening, at least on Sundays and feastdays, services are held; during the intervening hours, tourists are masters of the cathedrals and gaze at the religious fervor.

With regard to old Seibold and the object of our book, it would be a great help to know what goes on in the heads of tourists when they've entered the cathedrals. If their attitude were simply one of disdain and disrespect, the cathedrals would probably remain empty. If it were one of pious belief, there'd possibly be no tourism. Perhaps the tourists are like old Seibold: they have not fully come to grips with what they were told in their religious instruction, and so (as they travel, frequently by automobile) they find themselves searching for something they obviously do not find in the enjoyment of fish stew or in watching the flamenco dancers. Old Horkheimer and young Handke give the name "longing" to the feeling the tourists have.

If, despite the dissatisfaction with traditional religion, this longing is really, collectively there in an admittedly very vague form or even in a somewhat absurd form (amid the cameras and guidebooks), it does not prove that God exists. But it does serve as the basis for a critique of "reality," including the inevitability of death (!) and the definitive separation of lovers (through death) and the inability of lovers to communicate with each other even during life. It starts us thinking about unfulfillment, the inability of the things of our experience to satisfy us wholly, and doubts about reality (including the inevitability of death). (To think is to doubt, Wittgenstein tells us.)[16]

If the tourist feels such a longing in the dusk of dying day, then the bygone medieval religious fervor may really lay hold of him and not simply move him to melancholy. He may apprehend that fervor as unfinished business for him in the process of his becoming fully a man, there in the cathedral, after enjoying his technological, industrial fish stew.

Evidently, you must leave your car outside the cathedral. No entry except on foot.

14

Religious Instruction (Concluded)

Compare the following two texts:

1. On the evening of that first day of the week, even though the disciples had locked the doors of the place where they were for fear of the Jews, Jesus came and stood before them. "Peace be with you," he said.

When he had said this, he showed them his hands and his side. At the sight of the Lord the disciples rejoiced. "Peace be with you," he said again. . . .

Then he breathed on them and said: "Receive the Holy Spirit. If you forgive men's sins, they are forgiven them; if you hold them bound, they are held bound."

It happened that one of the Twelve, Thomas (the name means "Twin"), was absent when Jesus came. The other disciples kept telling him: "We have seen the Lord!"

His answer was, "I will never believe it without probing the nail-prints in his hands, without putting my finger in the nail-marks and my hand into his side."

A week later, the disciples were once more in the room, and this time Thomas was with them. Despite the locked doors, Jesus came and stood before them. "Peace be with you," he said; then, to Thomas: "Take your finger and examine my hands. Put your hand into my side. Do not persist in your unbelief, but believe!"

Thomas said in response, "My Lord and my God!"

(*This text is from the Bible.*)[1]

2. The young soldier Jean-Pierre Longchamp got his first leave and attended a ball. There he noticed a young girl in a white evening gown who could not find a seat, and he invited her to his table. Both were pleased. It was already long after midnight when Jean-Pierre asked his pretty dancing partner, Monique, how she had gotten the great scar on her right temple.

In an automobile accident two years before, she told him as she pressed her cheek to his. When the soldier brought Monique to her home, day was already dawning; she seemed in a hurry. Jean-Pierre put his coat around her shoulders to keep her warm against the chilly air of the morning. Before her door, a quick kiss; then she was gone.

Too late, Jean-Pierre realized she had kept his coat around her shoulders. But that gave him a good excuse to call the next day.

A man in his sixties opened the door, and was very angry when Jean-Pierre asked for Monique. "That's a rotten joke," he said, and started to slam the door. But then he saw that the young man was honestly surprised, and he said: "She died two years ago in an automobile accident, when I was taking her to her first ball."

Now Jean-Pierre told the father what had happened the night before. The man heard him through and said only, "The cemetery is close by."

The two went to the grave with the inscription: "Monique Maluint, 1954–1970." On the grave-slab lay Jean-Pierre's coat.

(*This text is from a newspaper.*)[2]

Indicate how the two texts are alike.
Indicate how they differ.
Is one of the two texts more credible than the other? Why?
Say: "Jesus, for you I live! Jesus, for you I die! Jesus, I am yours in life and in death!"

3. Inanna, the queen of heaven and the goddess of love, whom the shepherd Tammuz had wooed and wedded, decided to descend to the lower world, take power there, and raise the dead. The queen of the lower world was her older sister and bitter enemy, Ereshkigal, the Sumerian goddess of death and darkness.

Inanna reached her sister's throne, but there the judges of the dead looked at her and she became a corpse.

After three days and three nights her servant Ninshubur set out to get help for his mistress. After two vain attempts he obtained it from Enki, god of wisdom, who sent two aides with the food and water of life, and in fact Inanna was restored to life. She was allowed to return to the upper world, but in accordance with the rules of the lower world she had to provide a substitute for herself. The demons who accompanied her finally received her husband Tammuz as a victim; despite the intervention of Utu, the sun-god, Tammuz was carried to the underworld, and there he dwells still.
(*This text is a short version of the Sumerian myth of Inanna's descent to the underworld, from the second millennium before Christ.*)[3]

4. Starting from speculations on the beginning of life and from biological parallels, I drew the conclusion that, besides the instinct to preserve living substance and to join it into ever larger units, there must exist another, contrary instinct seeking to dissolve these units and to bring them back to their primeval, inorganic state. That is to say, as well as Eros there was an instinct of death. The phenomena of life could be explained from the concurrent or mutually opposing action of these two instincts.

It was not easy, however, to demonstrate the activities of this supposed death instinct. The manifestations of Eros were conspicuous and noisy enough. It might be assumed that the death instinct operated silently within the organism towards its dissolution, but that, of course, was no proof. A more fruitful idea was that a portion of the instinct is diverted towards the external world and comes to light as an instinct of aggressiveness and destructiveness. In this way the instinct itself could be pressed into the service of Eros, in that the organism was destroying some other thing, whether animate or inanimate, instead of destroying its own self. Conversely, any restriction of this aggressiveness directed outwards would be bound to increase the self-destruction, which is in any case proceeding. At the same time one can suspect from this example that the two kinds of instinct seldom—perhaps never—appear in isolation, but are alloyed with each other in varying and very different proportions and so become unrecognizable to our judgment.
(*This text is from Sigmund Freud's* Civilization and Its Discontents.)[4]

Compare and see how many similar statements are made in both texts. Is the comparison of Inanna with Eros, and of Ereshkigal with the death instinct, a valid one?

Ask yourself why the sisters, Inanna and Ereshkigal, must, in Freud's view, be hostile one to the other. Does the fourth text represent an advance in knowledge over the third? See the notes to this book for the correct answer.[5]

Ask yourself whether you felt anything when you spoke the words: "Jesus, for you I live! etc." If yes, what did you feel (for example, tenderness or revulsion)? If no, do you regret the fact? See whether you can put the four texts in a descending order, according to whether they are very important for your life, less important, of little importance, or totally unimportant (for example, 4, 1, 2, 3, or 1, 3, 4, 2, etc.).

If you found it possible to establish such an order, then ask yourself: Why was it possible?

If all four texts were equally important or equally unimportant to you, ask yourself: Why?

Is there any text that is the most important to you of all the texts you know?

If so, write it here:

____

____

____

If there is no such text, ask yourself: Why not?

N.B. *The texts can be of any kind you want.*

15

Much Light, and from All Directions

Please don't immediately say, "Ah, yes! that young hysteric back there, five hundred years ago!"

For, our inquiry into Easter brings us now to Joan of Arc, called "La Pucelle" ("The Maid"), who was born at Domrémy, France, in 1412, and died at the stake in Rouen, France, in 1431, on the Wednesday before Corpus Christi.

I also ask you, however, not to think immediately of Joan as wearing a halo (she was canonized by the Catholic Church in 1920).

We are engaged, after all, in an inquiry; for that we need the detective frame of mind and therefore a certain sobriety and the kind of accurate observation one brings to the study of a report on a trial. The minutes of the trial at which Joan was condemned and of the later trial at which she was rehabilitated still exist in the original manuscript; they have been published, commented on by scholars, and translated.

But why turn to Joan in the quest for light to guide our steps? Why not to Angela Davis, for example, or to Jesus? Well, as far as Jesus is concerned, there's already been a great deal written on him (by this writer, among others), and, besides, Jesus is very much present at the trial of Joan, and in a very appropriate way—as the name the doomed criminal cries out when the pyre is lit.

The whole business of Angela Davis, on the other hand, is too chancy to waste a lot of words on it here; the same holds for the lady from Prague.

In any event we have deliberately made a woman the object of our Easter inquiry so that we won't have to be dealing again with an important leader. (We can't forget, of course, that Joan has become a national heroine, but that fact is not important here.)

In addition, there is a bit of the atmosphere of the sporting world about Joan, when we consider the brevity and rapidity of her public career (in this she also resembles Jesus). In January, 1429, she left home, in February gained access to the Dauphin at Chinon, in May and June conducted a campaign that drove the English from the Loire Valley, and in July led the Dauphin to his coronation at Rheims. At this point she was forced to delay awhile; she would have preferred to attack Paris (it was the king who hesitated). In April, 1430, she advanced on Compiègne, in May was betrayed, captured, and sold to the English, and in December was brought to Rouen. The trial began in February, 1431, and Joan was dead by the end of May.

Joan did accomplish something: she shifted the balance (in France's favor) in the so-called Hundred Years' War between France and England. In her case, then, there is no element of Dr. Freud's lullaby, mentioned earlier. A real historical force was at work in her, and because this Easter force has still not won out over death and the devil (but is not therefore any less real than UNF), the five hundred and fifty years that have passed since then are not very important in this context. In fact, the passage of such a long period of time is an advantage to the researcher. For, the camouflage adopted by Joan's enemies (reasons of State, and so forth) has worn away over the years, and we can see the real situation more clearly than the people of the time could. Bishops' miters and academic titles no longer lend respectability to the darkened and distorted thinking of that day, and only Joan now stands bathed in light.

EASTER LITURGY

Joan's trial has liturgical overtones. It begins on the Wednesday after the First Sunday of Lent and ends on the Wednesday before Corpus Christi. Priests conduct it; Easter comes halfway through. During the trial Joan asks often and urgently for a confessor and for Communion, especially on Easter; both are granted her only on the morning of her execution.

So that we may have an accurate picture and that those unfamiliar with the liturgical calendar may not be at sea, we shall outline the sequence of events (the lefthand column gives the liturgical calendar, the righthand the events of the trial).

The year: 1431

February	*February*
17 First Sunday of Lent	
	21 First public interrogation
	22 Second public interrogation
	24 Third public interrogation
25 Second Sunday of Lent	
	27 Fourth public interrogation
March	*March*
	1 Fifth public interrogation
	3 Sixth public interrogation
4 Third Sunday of Lent	
	10 First secret interrogation
11 Fourth Sunday of Lent	
	12 Second and third secret interrogations
	13 Fourth secret interrogation
	14 Fifth and sixth secret interrogations

	15 Seventh secret interrogation
	17 Eighth and ninth secret interrogations
18 Passion Sunday	Deliberations of the judges
25 Palm Sunday	Exhortation to the accused
	27 Presentation of the articles of accusation
	28 Reading of the accusations
Holy Saturday	31 Final interrogation
April	*April*
1 Easter Sunday	
2 Easter Monday	Deliberations
8 Quasimodo Sunday	
15 Second Sunday after Easter	
	18 Admonition to the accused
22 Third Sunday after Easter	
29 Fourth Sunday after Easter	
May	*May*
	2 Second admonition to the accused
6 Fifth Sunday after Easter	
	9 Threat of torture
10 Ascension Thursday	
13 Sixth Sunday after Easter	
	19 Reading of the opinions of the University of Paris
20 Pentecost Sunday	
	23 Second reading of the same. Reading of the twelve points of guilt. Further sermon of exhortation
	24 First pronouncement of sentence. Recantation by the accused Second pronouncement of sentence (lifelong imprisonment)

May	*May*
27 Feast of the Most Blessed Trinity	
	28 Verification of relapse of the accused; single interrogation
	29 Deliberation on the relapse; sentence
	30 Execution of sentence
31 Corpus Christi	

(The liturgical calendar is still the same, even after the Reformation; trials today do not follow the same form as they did then.)

SHE MADE VERY FINE REPLIES

In February, 1450, King Charles VII wrote to Guillaume Bouillé, one of his councillors and Rector of the University of Paris since 1439. This letter gave the first official impetus to a retrial with a view to rehabilitating Joan. An appeal was addressed to the Pope, who ordered a trial of vindication, in the course of which about one hundred and fifty witnesses were called.

Among the witnesses were some who had sat in judgment on Joan in 1431 and consented to her condemnation; for example, the respected Jean Tiphaine, priest, Master of Arts and Medicine, Canon of the Royal Chapel at Paris, whose testimony was taken on April 2, 1456, when he was sixty years old. Tiphaine says he can't remember having ever expressed the slightest opinion on the trial, except with respect to an illness of Joan while she was in prison. (But his signature is found on the original manuscript of the death sentence.)

Tiphaine says: "I did not know Joan until she was brought to Rouen for trial. The first time I was asked to attend her I refused to go. But when I was asked a second time I went and watched, and listened to the questions and her replies. She made very fine replies." [1]

Tiphaine mentions—and he is not the only one to do so—his fear of the English: "The first time that I was called for this case I refused to go, and the second time I went because I was afraid of the English, . . . so that I should not thereby incur their anger." [2]

Tiphaine is not the only one to marvel (in the safety of a later day) at the intelligence of Joan who could not read or write and stood all alone before an illustrious court. (The president is Msgr. Pierre Cauchon, Bishop of Beauvais, Doctor of Sacred Theology, Master of Arts, etc. On the bench with him is the Reverend Jean d'Estivet, spiritual counselor, Canon of Beauvais and Bayeux, and prosecutor at the trial. Among the forty-three assessors are many abbots and priors of famous monasteries, canons, secular priests, and monks.) Trick questions were put to Joan; the interrogations sometimes went on for several hours; the court record was left incomplete (this was deliberate to some extent). Joan remembers her own past statements exactly; she corrects the court reporters, she fights with persevering alertness, sometimes makes tactical concessions, never betrays herself, and it is only the sight of the executioners that causes her to become afraid, so that on May 29 she recants, but even then she is in good humor (several eyewitnesses mention how she laughed at the moment).

Joan's intelligence is in fact radiant and contrasts with the average feeble intellectual powers of her judges (recall Dr. Freud's remark quoted in chapter 5). Bishop Cauchon in person conducts the first public interrogation. He calls upon Joan to say the Our Father. Joan: "Hear my confession and I'll be glad to say it for you." (She thus appeals to the priest in her judge and wants to make her case a matter of conscience; the Our Father has nothing to do with the trial.) Cauchon: "You have tried frequently to escape from other prisons; that is why we have put you in chains—to keep you in sure custody." Joan: "Yes, I have tried to escape from other prisons and I'd do it now if I could. Every prisoner has the right to escape." [3]

(The validity of this principle has not been accepted even today.)

The voices which guide Joan become the subject of interrogation beginning with the second public session.[4]

JOAN: "When I was thirteen, a voice from God spoke to me to guide me. The first time I was very afraid. The voice came at noon, on a Sunday, in my father's garden. I had fasted the day before. I heard the voice on my right, from the direction of the church."

JUDGE: "Do you see a light when you hear the voice?"

JOAN: "There is almost always a great brightness with it. The light comes from the same side as the voice. Usually I see a bright light there."

JUDGE: "Was the voice that of an angel? Or a male saint? Or a woman saint? Was it the voice of God himself or of a go-between?" (The fourth interrogation deals almost exclusively with the voice; the judge wants to know all about it in detail.)

JOAN: "It was the voices of St. Catherine and St. Margaret. On their heads they wore beautiful, rich, costly crowns. God gave me permission to say that much." (Gradually Joan gives detailed information; she repeatedly asserts, however, that all this has nothing to do with the trial.)

JUDGE: "Did you ever embrace St. Catherine and St. Margaret?"

JOAN: "Yes, I embraced them both."

JUDGE: "Did they smell good?"

JOAN: "Of course, they did! I could not embrace them without smelling and touching them."

JUDGE: "When you saw your voices, was there any light?"[5]

JOAN: "Much light, and from all directions, as was right and proper. Not near so much has come to you!"

THE WEAK POINT

After her recantation Joan makes a request: "And now, gentlemen of the Church, put me into your prison, so that I may no longer be in the hands of the English." Bishop Cauchon replies: "Take her back whence you brought her." [6]

So we are told by the senior clerk of the court, Guillaume Manchon, who was one of the most important witnesses at the trial of rehabilitation. (He and two others were responsible for the minutes of the trials. On the points that concern us his testimony is supported by other witnesses.) Manchon gives the reason for Joan's request:

> Joan was asked during the trial why she did not wear women's clothing, since, as the questioners said, it was improper for a woman to wear a coat of mail and trousers. In reply, I heard Joan complain to the Bishop and the Earl of Warwick. She explained that she wouldn't dare leave off wearing trousers or not keep them laced up tightly, because, as the Bishop and the Earl were well aware, the guards had frequently tried to rape her. One day, in fact, the Earl had come to help her when he heard her screams. If he had not come, the guards would have overpowered her.[7]

Another witness, Jean Massieu (master, priest, clerk of the court) describes what happened after the recantation:

> After dinner that day, she put off her male clothes . . . and put on women's clothes, as she had been ordered to. . . . Her male clothes were put in a sack in her prison room.[8]
>
> Joan was kept a prisoner and remained in that place under the guard of five Englishmen, of whom three stayed in her room at night and two remained outside the door. And I know for certain that at night she lay chained by the legs with two pairs of irons, and tightly secured by another chain which passed through the legs of her bed, and was attached to a great

block of wood five or six feet long, by means of a lock. In this way she was unable to stir from her place.[9]

On the following Sunday morning, which was Trinity Sunday, when it was time for her to get up she said to her English guards, as she told me: "Take off my chains. I am going to get up." Then one of the Englishmen pulled off the women's clothing that covered her and they emptied the sack in which were her male clothes. These they flung to her, saying, "Get up," and stowed her women's clothes in the bag. But first she said: "Sirs, you know very well that this is forbidden me. I will not wear them." Nevertheless they refused to give her any other clothes, and the argument went on till noon. Finally, she was compelled to go out—in order to fulfill a physical need—and to wear these clothes. When she came back they still refused to give her any others, notwithstanding all her demands and supplications.[10]

Finally, the truth, the everyday truth, comes out. On the next day, Monday, the panel of judges appears in the prison and certifies that Joan is wearing men's clothes again; on Tuesday they declare her relapsed, and on Wednesday hand her over to the executioners. Witnesses report that on that Monday Msgr. Cauchon, at the end of the session, laughed and said to the Earl of Warwick and the other Englishmen: "Be of good cheer, she is ours now!" [11]

Joan's weak point, her theological weak point, is between her thighs.

As long as males can laugh in the way just mentioned, things do not look good for eternal life. (Joan laughed too, at her recantation, as we mentioned earlier. But it was quite a different kind of laugh, quite different!)

This kind of male laughter springs from the Id (see Dr. Freud!). Msgr. Cauchon feels impelled to laugh. Laughter rises up in him.

There is a lesson to be learned from Lord Bishop Cauchon, but what is it? Love and death are sisters who hate each other and are locked in endless struggle in the underworld. The day after tomorrow the Maid will burn, and Cauchon feels impelled to laugh. (Cauchon is reported as looking on at the execution, while the other judges left.)

From the psychic caverns of the Cauchons (*cochons?* See your French dictionary!) something foreboding makes its presence known—something that refuses to die, wants to live on and outlive everyone else. Cauchon wants to survive; he acts out of fear of the English, and Joan must burn.

There is a Cauchon in all of us; this is confirmed by the material psychoanalysis provides.[12] The unconscious as seat of the pleasure principle does not acknowledge the category of time, but thinks of itself as eternal; it is convinced of its own immortality. It laughs, and as long as it continues to laugh we should be a little careful about our yearnings for immortality.

Joan, innocent victim of the desire of her judges (and of the Earl of Warwick and the English) to survive, speaks to her murderers of St. Catherine and St. Margaret who visit her. She speaks hesitantly and reluctantly because she is addressing her murderers. (Please don't think of this account as simply a criticism of the Church; murderers, after all, don't *have* to wear a bishop's miter.) Joan is embarrassed only because there are murderers present; she is not at all embarrassed by St. Catherine and St. Margaret, since she takes their company for granted.

Whether St. Catherine and St. Margaret come from the same place as Cauchon's laughter is a theological question we may raise here and answer with a no.

We must also remember that the murderers triumphed over their innocent victim for only a short time, and then only by making use of her weak point. Joan won out over her murderers after her death, and no cock has to crow any more at them.

The sensible elements in Joan's visions (seeing, hearing, smelling) are just as real as her political and military accomplishments and just as real as her posthumous victory over her murderers. Her voices (along with the beautiful crowns and the good smell) assure her that at the end she will reach paradise.

JOAN: "I firmly believe that I shall be saved, as my voices promised. I believe it as firmly as if I were already there."
JUDGE: "A very important answer!" [13]

In this case we can agree unreservedly with the judge.

PROFESSIONS OF FAITH

We should note that St. Catherine and St. Margaret did not come to King Charles VII but to Joan, a peasant's daughter who could not read or write. We should note that an assurance of paradise, including light ("much light") and odor ("a good smell"), was given to little Joan during her lifetime and not to her high and mighty judges, who would put no credence at all in her. Considering these facts, we begin to suspect that you don't reach paradise if you're arrogant and conceited. Our inquiries thus lead to a conclusion that will please old Seibold.

Our suspicion is that UNF talks too much about God and paradise, and that the attitudes and language of UNF have cornered the market in theological thought—and we've believed the silly stuff! It is, after all, from the sphere of juridical power that the conviction comes that we can pass judgment with regard to paradise. Tribunals reach the judgments, while Joan smells the good odor of St. Catherine and St. Margaret.

We suspect, moreover, that concepts are related to police activity, that is, to grasping, laying hands on, seizing.[14] Joan has no desire to seize St. Catherine and St. Margaret; she just tenderly embraces them at the knees (as she says in the minutes).

There is no spiritism here, since Joan has received a real task to be done in the here and now, for the sake of her people, and she has executed the task as best she could.

From below, then, that is, from Joan, judgment is passed on the judges: the seizers, the concept-makers and judgers, the wordsmiths who serve kings and majesties and pyramid-builders with all their almighty and majestic gods and great lords and all their bombast and theatrical effects laid on for the people who look up and tremble with pleasure and are filled with sorrow and raise tearful hands. Or else they are allowed to go on an automobile trip and spend three weeks' vacation in Barcelona, so that they can boast of some acquaintance with the wide world and therefore a degree of personal importance. Paradise, meanwhile, is won elsewhere with St. Catherine and St. Margaret (much light and a good odor).

Perhaps at this point we may suggest a new way of addressing God; St. Augustine will surely forgive us for the correction. He begins the thirteen books of his *Confessions* by telling God: "You are great, O Lord." We recommend beginning with "You are little, O Lord."

In regard to professions of faith: The profession of faith used in the early Church may be traced back, as in Joan's case, to the courtroom, where the Roman judges used to interrogate accused Christians. (Some of the Acts of the Martyrs that have come down to us are genuine.) When Christianity later became the official religion, the profession of faith turned into a set of sentiments drawn up by the authorities and was marked by a certain solemn triumphalism (you can hear the kettledrums and trumpets in the background). The Roman judges acquired the miter of Catholic bishops and the title of teacher, and sat again in judgment, but this time on the faith (as in the case of Joan), and even commanded that the Our Father be said in orderly fashion (UNF!). (The lady in Prague is well acquainted with this sort of thing; the judges have simply changed hats again.)

The poor little faith is at a disadvantage from the beginning, since it must speak and answer as one accused. The good odor of St. Catherine and St. Margaret must be perceived and judged by the authorities; Joan's paradise is documented. The perfume of hope in the face of death and the devil fades in the process like ink on old paper; the beauty of St. Catherine and St. Margaret, that was so real and sensible, literally evaporates into the air, and what is left is a profession of faith.

The judges' questions (was there a light? did they smell good?) betrays a rather intimate knowledge of Joan's heavenly joy. The knowledge surprises us, because Joan was very careful and gave away only what she absolutely had to.

So then: was there a spy at work?

Manchon, the clerk we have already quoted, tells us:

> When Boisguillaume and I were appointed clerks for the trial, the Earl of Warwick, the Bishop of Beauvais, and Master Nicholas Loiseleur told us that Joan was making astounding statements about her visions and that in order to get at the truth a plan had been concocted. Master Nicholas was to pretend to be a fellow prisoner from Lorraine, Joan's own country, and an adherent of the king. He was to get into her cell in the short dress of a layman; the watch would withdraw and he would be alone with her.
>
> But in the wall of the next cell an opening had been made. We were to hide behind it and listen to what Joan might say. And, in fact, the Earl and I went there, and Joan could not see us. Loiseleur told Joan all sorts of stories about the king and her revelations to him, and Joan talked to Loiseleur as to a fellow countryman who was loyal to the king. The Bishop and the Earl had ordered Boisguillaume and me to write down her answers. I refused on the grounds that it was improper to begin a trial with that sort of trick. Joan put great trust in Loiseleur from the very beginning.[15]

(Manchon's testimony is substantially confirmed by Boisguillaume, his fellow clerk.)

The spy, then, is Nicholas Loiseleur, who later signed the death sentence; he is a priest and master, and blows hot and cold. He wants to serve these grand gentlemen, but at the same time seems to want to help Joan: perhaps he can save her from the worst. Boisguillaume says that Loiseleur almost went out of his wits when he saw her condemned to death; he asked her forgiveness and even jumped into the executioner's cart to do so.[16] Warwick advised him to disappear from Rouen as quickly as possible if he valued his life; he died at Basel.

The mysteries associated with Joan's faith were thus made known even before the trial began. She had to make some concessions, therefore, and admit what she had experienced with regard to paradise. In the judgment of the court all this was nothing but heresy, witchcraft, and sorcery. Here again, the pearls were cast before swine. The judges managed to poison the wells from which Joan drew pure water; terrorism in the hands of authority has subtle means at its disposal.

The testimony at the trial of rehabilitation ends with a statement from Jean Riquier, priest and chaplain at Rouen. Riquier had not taken part in the trial but he tells of a conversation between Joan and a Master Pierre on the morning of the execution.

> Master Pierre Maurice visited her that morning, before she was led to the sermon in the Vieux Marché; and Joan said to him: "Master Pierre, where shall I be tonight?" And Master Pierre answered her: "Do you not trust in God?" She said that she did and that, with God's aid, she would be in Paradise. This I have from Master Pierre himself. When Joan saw the fire set to the wood, she began to cry aloud, "Jesus, Jesus!" and right up to her death she went on crying, "Jesus!" [17]

16

Transubstantiation

First, hosts have to be brought.

It is 1945, and the server is bringing hosts. The war is over; the Great Powers have entered Vienna. In the fourteenth ward (parish church of St. Lawrence), as elsewhere, foreign soldiers may be seen. I have a knapsack and in it an empty cardboard box for the hosts; our hosts are gotten in a convent in the tenth ward; the Sisters in Alxingergasse bake hosts after the war and fill my box for me.

Hosts weigh little, they are made of wheat flour and water, without yeast, and then baked quickly. The composition of the hosts is like that of the Jewish matzos which are used at Passover. Christians call Passover Easter, and matzos hosts. Before the war many Jews, Dr. Freud among them, used to live in Vienna; after the war there were no more Jews in Vienna.

I carry the hosts to the St. Lawrence parish house. On the park benches I see: "Aryans only."

Without the hosts (the Latin *hostia* means "victim") there is no Consecration.

Elias Canetti tells us: "In 1924 I attended the University of Vienna and spent my evenings writing. I was a little over twenty at the time when one day, on the street, I first got the idea of writing a book on crowds. It was like a revelation. I decided to devote my life to the study of crowds." [1]

He continues:

> The Nazis came to Vienna in 1938, and although all my friends strongly urged me to leave, I couldn't bring myself to do it immediately, despite the danger I was in as an intellectual of Jewish descent. I stayed until "Crystal Night" at the end of November, 1938. During that half year I went everywhere—on the streets, in the shops—and talked to the people I met. And I would say that during those six months of down to earth experience I learned more about National Socialism than I had in all the years before.[2]

The ciborium holds about three hundred hosts, which are later distributed to the faithful. (The priest's host is somewhat larger than the hosts given to the people.) The hosts are placed in the ciborium beforehand in the sacristy; the server puts them in carefully, layer on layer.

That's how I learn to handle hosts.

It's an honor and a sign of trust that a server is allowed to put the hosts in the ciborium. For, it's a rule that only priests may touch the sacred vessels. Consequently, a server is in awe of sacred vessels and of the hosts too; we may speak in this context of a phobia about touching—the kind of thing we read about in studies of primitive peoples.

The server must learn that the godhead is fearsome. Anything that comes in contact with the godhead must be handled with great awe and caution. The inside of the ciborium is gilded, because it comes in contact with the godhead.

The Germans have no Führer now. He died in Berlin in 1945. I lay the hosts carefully in the golden ciborium.

Canetti says:

> I've attempted to show that the main feeling associated with power springs from the living person's sense of triumph over the dead person lying there before him. It is a simple fact that everyone who survives another feels a sense of triumph because he is still alive; this is true whether or not he admits to the feeling. (Usually he won't, because it is rightly regarded as an ugly feeling.) In many people this feeling of triumph becomes a kind of passion that calls for constant repetition. The most dangerous politicians, especially the fascist politicians of our time, are men who need and demand death on a massive scale. The more dead people—enemies or even friends—they survive, the more intense their sense of power.[3]

Wicked old UNF (N as in Neanderthal, F as in Fascist) has a host in his hand, and heavy rings on his fingers. On his head he wears a triple crown. He's been there for everyone to see since 1510 on the pulpit of St. Stephan's Cathedral in Vienna: a bitter old fellow with a thin mouth, his eyes looking past the host. He doesn't believe in the redemption. He's made of stone.

The server will make his acquaintance later on. For the time being, he places small round white hosts in the golden ciborium, reverently and lovingly.

Matzos and hosts can be thought of as vegetarian food. The unleavened bread has no links with cattle raising or hunting or the eating of the flesh of slain animals. Its connections are with agriculture and the agricultural customs of prehistoric Canaan (Palestine).

In this context we will recall one of old Seibold's questions (chapter 9, above): "Isn't the claim of every single being in this world a valid one? Why must the animals of our earth live on other animals and vegetation, and we men on animals and vegetation?"

Canetti, too, views man's feeding habits with deep mistrust: "Why must flesh be constantly passing through the intestines of another's flesh?"[4]

In his book *Crowds and Power* Canetti offers some very penetrating and distressing observations on eating:

> The actual *incorporation* of the prey begins in the mouth. From hand to mouth is the route followed by everything which can be eaten. . . . The most striking natural instrument of power in man and in many animals is the teeth. The way they are arranged in rows and their shining smoothness are quite different from anything else belonging to the body. One is tempted to call them the very first manifestation of order and one so striking that it almost shouts for recognition. It is an order which operates as a threat to the world outside, not always visible, but visible whenever the mouth opens, which is often. . . . *Smoothness* and *order,* the manifest attributes of the teeth, have entered into the very nature of power. . . . The teeth are the armed guardians of the mouth and the mouth is indeed a strait place, the prototype of all prisons. Whatever goes in there is lost. . . . The road the prey travels through the body is a long one and on the way all its substance is sucked out of it; everything useful is abstracted from it till all that remains is refuse and stench.[5]

When the Mass reaches the stage of Communion, the server is the first to receive the host from the priest. Each day the priest lays a little white host on my tongue. (Only the priest may touch the hosts with his hand when he distributes them to the faithful at Mass.) The server tries not to touch the host with his teeth. He lets it soften on his tongue and then swallows it.

The server thus learns what is special about this type of eating. He learns that here we have an attempt to find an exception to the rule that food must pass through our intestines. The nutritional value of the host is so slight that it sets the digestive system in motion only in a minimal degree. The host lacks, as far as this is possible, the aspect of prey that goes with other foods.

> Even the very way in which the communion is administered separates each believer from the others who receive it with him, instead of there and then uniting them. The communicant receives a precious treasure for himself. It is for himself that he expects it, and for himself that he must guard it. If one observes those waiting for communion it is impossible not to be struck by the fact that each individual is occupied exclusively with himself. The person in front of and behind him matters even less to him than a fellow human being in ordinary life; and that is little enough. The communion links the recipient with the vast, invisible Church, but it detaches him from those actually present. Among themselves the communicants feel as little one body as a group of men who have found treasure and just divided it between them.[6]

Canetti, whom we have just been quoting, notes, as a disinterested observer, the care the priest uses in distributing the hosts. The server accompanies him, holding a golden plate under the chins of the faithful, lest a host accidentally fall to the floor. When the distribution of Communion is finished, the server must bring the plate to the altar so that the priest may clean it. Not the tiniest fragment of a host must be allowed to be lost. The priest then locks the ciborium with the remaining hosts in a little box at the center of the altar. In the parish church of St. Lawrence this place of reservation is in the shape of an armored cupboard. I know that I am forbidden even to put the key in the lock.

The rules for handling hosts are universal and very strict. Behind them lurks a deep distrust on the part of the priest: thieves may come and steal the golden ciborium, and in the process carelessly dump out the hosts (tales of this kind of thing are told with a shudder). God must be protected from men. Only priests are authorized to turn the key in the lock of the armored box that contains the hosts. The authority of the faithful with regard to the host is almost nonexistent: they may only extend their tongues for it.

Thus the server learns a lot about matters human and divine and about the powers that come into play. For him, all power is concentrated in the host, and he begins to wish that he might belong to the privileged circle of those authorized to handle it. For, the right to handle the host brings an immense share of power. Anyone who wants to exercise this power must undergo very strict tests, among the most important of which is chastity. It is unthinkable that a man should successively touch the body of Christ and the body of a woman. Even to think of it would be a serious sin for the server. Serious sin is also called deadly sin. Death lies in wait for anyone who deals lightly with the host.

I used to be especially happy on solemn feastdays. Then the walls of the sanctuary would be covered with rich, sound-muffling tapestries; rugs covered the floor out to the barrier at the people's side (the Communion rail, as it was called). The church of St. Lawrence is in the Gothic style; the altar is in the sanctuary where only the priests and servers may go, and the faithful stay out in the nave which is at a lower level than the sanctuary.

Within the sanctuary further steps lead up to the altar, which is also called the high altar to distinguish it from the other and less important altars in the church. On the high altar sits the safe with the hosts in it. The red-tapestried walls of the sanctuary and the white rugs on the floor give the server a special feeling of happiness on solemn feastdays. There are the slow deliberate movements; the precise ceremonies of the High Mass; the organ music that swells out mightily as the officiants enter the sanctuary on solemn feastdays; the powerful music of many voices and instruments in the Kyrie, Gloria, Credo, Sanctus, and Agnus Dei. The servers are robed in red and white, the priests in gold and white. Many servers and several priests offer their services to the host on solemn feastdays in the brightly lit, red-tapestried sanctuary. The latter is smaller than the nave and gives the server a feeling of security and even of rapture.

The server seems to himself to be in another world; our present world lies out there beyond the Communion rail where the lights are dimmer and the atmosphere less fervid. During High Mass little heed is paid that world of the faithful, and then only at odd moments, by those in the other world of the sanctuary. The latter is the place of the chaste; here they are rewarded. Women and girls must stay in our present world and not join the priests and servers.

The distribution of the hosts takes place at a low railing that divides the sanctuary from the rest of the church. It is called the Communion rail. Being a server, I stand on the other-world side of the Communion rail; women and girls must stay beyond the barrier. They come forward humbly to Communion but may never cross the critical barrier. Sometimes a server will press the golden plate against a girl's throat at Communion; he does it in jest, but it is forbidden. But the girls know what's what and give no hint, but keep their eyes down. After Communion has been distributed the server turns his back on the girls again.

"Communion" is from the Latin word *communis,* that is, "shared."

The steps up the altar lead away from other people.

And upward, to a superior place.

I wanted to reach that place so that I might at last be alone with the host, alone at the center of power for all eternity. An inflexible will to immortality, like that of the pharaohs, a will to be apart, is what turns the key in the lock of the armored box on the altar. Hosts are handled like gold pieces even today; the dead Jesus preaches to the souls of the children with tears streaming down his face, but seemingly in vain. Seemingly in vain the priests raise the host aloft, seemingly in vain are the words of the dead Jesus repeated: "This is my body for you."

It is at this point that the consecration/transubstantiation takes place.

The authorized person (priest, pastor, pope, etc.) has the function of effecting transubstantiation by repeating the words I just quoted, at a predetermined point in time of which the public knows, usually in the context of an assembly in a church. Bread (hosts) is necessary. Immediately after the consecration of the bread, wine is changed into the blood of Christ; this act, too, originates with Jesus. That the transubstantiation may be effected only by authorized persons is a conclusion reached in the course of the first Christian centuries; this development is irreversible.

The presence of personnel authorized to consecrate belongs (as do power and majesty and armored box and Gothic style and organs and steps to the high altar, and so on) to the human sphere; transubstantiation itself belongs to the divine.

The inevitability of death (along with avalanches, floods, the passion for automobiles, tourism, blossoming flowers, cancer, the universe, etc.) belongs to the human sphere. Despair over the human sphere and its arrangements can at times, but only momentarily, lead men to acknowledge the presence of the divine world. It makes sense to describe the attitude to transubstantiation as a despairing of the human world and its arrangements.

The human world and the divine are both present.

We must not confuse the two in our thinking.

We must not think of them as separated.

We must not neglect the one for the sake of the other.

The following statements are meaningful and useful: We secretly accept the deaths of others; we cannot accept our own death. Both attitudes are reprehensible, and a change in them is to be desired. Transubstantiation can change our habitual attitudes to death.

Transubstantiation presupposes the death of the person involved, for, as a result of it his body is given to others as food so that they may live. The point, the penetrating judgment implicit in this act, should not be missed. It goes directly to the core of the evil in us, namely, our will to assert ourselves by devouring others and feeding on them. The evil is healed by being permitted to happen—in a tolerable way, that is, in the eating of the consecrated host.

The cannibalism inherent in human relations and thus the will to survive at the expense of others is made evident and also cured in the consecration/transubstantiation. He who loses his life shall gain it. Joan's dying cry illustrates this principle.

Consecration and communion form a coherent whole. Communion is sometimes illustrated by the image of a certain bird feeding its young. The bird is the pelican, and the special manner in which it feeds its young gave people long ago the impression it was feeding them with its own blood.

It is amazing what freshness and original power the consecration/transubstantiation still has, despite the mystifications with which it has been surrounded. Realism and openness to new possibilities seem to join hands in it. It is as though the ultimate reaches of human possibility were anticipated in it.

Is old Seibold, then, when all is said and done, to be sent back to the Church? Am I to stir up his piety in his old age with pastoral gestures that have become increasingly impotent?

No, he's quite familiar already with all the ecclesiastical display.

The important thing is rather to intensify old Seibold's ability to discern the successful transubstantiations that take place here and there and to be unwearyingly sensitive to the nameless joy that fills the (rare) moments when the chains fall away (the kind of joy hinted at in Beethoven's music for *Fidelio*). And I don't mean just in the opera house or just in the church, but when the wood is lit and little Joan triumphs over death and the devil. (?) (!)

We who are in positions of authority become men of little faith because of our office; it is the unauthorized who work the miracles. Our resistance to change is great; we're skeptical about transubstantiation taking place.

The opportunity for the unauthorized, on the other hand, comes in the change of relationships, in transubstantiation; unfortunately, the unauthorized are hesitant about accepting this (if they accept it at all). In many cases, we manage to prevent the unauthorized from really believing in transubstantiation. Something in them connives with us in our efforts: a submissiveness that has its roots far back in the past.

It says a great deal for the historical force of the consecration/transubstantiation that it hasn't faded into thin air in our hands. By great good fortune, one or other of the authorized rediscovers himself to be one of the unauthorized; the consecration itself has detached him from reliance on his authorization.

The greater the number of the authorized who descend the steps of their respective altars, the sooner death will lose its sting.

In spotting successful transubstantiations we must be on guard against being deceived by the naturalistic pattern of dying-and-rising (*Stirb-und-Werde*); that only hinders a true understanding of the divine world. The study of nature at the microscopic and macroscopic levels (even, and especially, in the present state of knowledge) brings to light, in fact, a large element of the unintentional, even the accidental, and therefore of fatalism. The (biological) concept of mutation is worlds removed from the concept of transubstantiation. So, the quasi-eternal cycle of the seasons (winter storms followed by May moons, etc.) will shed no light on transubstantiation.

Transubstantiation intervenes in the natural processes, but with clear purpose and always with seeming unsuccess.

The authorities (or UNF), on the other hand, incline to fatalism about the laws at work in natural events, including human relationships.

As we can see, old Seibold must be put on guard against all sorts of illusions, even in the discussion of transubstantiation (or eternal life, as the case may be).

In July 1969 I watched the television in Aigues-Mortes and saw the first flight of two men to the moon. It was a kind of realistic Ascension, at least for Werner von Braun, according to whom this "new attainment . . . brings us nearer to the heavens."[7]

Norman Mailer has described his feelings as he walked through the Vehicle Assembly Building at Cape Kennedy. He speaks of "the first cathedral in the age of technology" and observes: "the world had changed."[8]

It is instructive to compare this sort of change with transubstantiation. The comparison shows that our age has a deep interest in changes. Change depends on technology, science, and economics, and thus on industry (and the bureaucracy that is part of it). It also depends on production, or mass production, in which UNF plays an eager part, as can be seen from the first rockets that were launched on London under Hitler in a real act of progress; it can also be seen in such modern developments as antirocket rockets with atomic warheads.

Yet, according to Mailer, the workers in the Vehicle Assembly Building at Cape Kennedy had happy faces, and the days before the launch were like the week before Christmas.[9]

Was there, then, a moment of success at the end of the countdown ("Stay! You are so lovely!")? The fulfillment of a possibility that had earlier seemed impossible? A reason for a Alleluia? Had something new been wrested or cunningly stolen or bullied from nature? Was it a victory for the spirit of enterprise? A bet won? A breakthrough to the stars—perhaps even inhabited stars—by astronauts with obedient computers as their indispensable helpers? The beginning of a new eon? A space age born when Saturn V and Apollo XI came alive with golden flames and thunderous explosions?

Transubstantiation

I no longer remember what I had to drink in the little bar where the television set was, during that 1969 vacation in Aigues-Mortes. I no longer remember my reactions to the television image of two men walking on the moon. I understood hardly anything of the commentary. My thoughts were still in Lourdes, where we had been two days before and where I had said Mass while the three astronauts were on their way to the moon.

My problem is to find some connection between my looking at the transubstantiated host at Lourdes and my looking at the moon-walk of Armstrong and Aldrin on the television set at Aigues-Mortes. Both were momentary glances. Time stood still. (President Nixon telephoned the moon from the White House and used the phrase, "For one priceless moment.")[10]

I must have my eyes tested.

The moment of transubstantiation requires good eyesight.

At the consecration the priest takes the host in his hands and speaks the words of transubstantiation. Then he shows the host to the congregation.

Between consecration and communion my eyes sometimes rest on the consecrated host. I see no sign of change; my eyes are conceivably unsuited for perceiving the transubstantiation. Yet, now and then, there seem to be moments when my gaze penetrates the host and gets lost within it as though I were inside a great vault. I really do get that feeling, and I'd be quite reluctant to suppress it. I can't teach others, even close friends, how to acquire it. It is more important to me than the sight of two men on the moon as seen on the television screen.

For me the transubstantiation is more real than the landing on the moon; the landing on the moon has not changed the capacity of my eyes to see.

I left Aigues-Mortes in the late morning. The moon was waxing.

Notes

CHAPTER 1

1. *Confiteor* ("I confess . . .") and *Suscipiat* ("May the Lord receive . . .") are the opening words of some prayers in the Roman Mass. The Roman liturgy was gradually revised during the 1960s and use of the vernacular was allowed; the reform is still going on.

2. Maurice Merleau-Ponty, *Adventures of the Dialectic*, translated by Joseph Bien (Evanston, 1973), p. 53.

3. "How I love your dwelling place, (O Lord of Hosts)!" (Ps. 83:1 Vulgate).

4. Alfred Döblin, *Berlin Alexanderplatz*, translated by Eugene Jolas (New York: Ungar, 1958). The second sentence is from p. 632. [I have not been able to find the first sentence in the English translation and have translated it from the German as given by Holl.—Tr.]

5. "The sparrow finds itself a house" (Ps. 83:4 Vulgate); "We will go into the house of the Lord" (Ps. 121:1 Vulgate).

6. Philip Marlowe is the hero in most of the stories by Raymond Chandler (died 1959). The best of them seems to me to be *The Long Goodbye*, in which the strange lady appears at evening.

7. T. S. Eliot, *The Waste Land* (1922).

8. "Direct, we beseech you, O Lord, all our actions by your holy inspiration. . . ."

9. Hans Pfitzner, *Palestrina: Musikalische Legende in drei Akten*, act 1, scene 3.

10. Ibid., scene 5.

11. Max Scheler, *On the Eternal in Man*, translated by Bernard Noble (New York: Harper, 1960), p. 107.

12. Vatican II, *Pastoral Constitution on the Church in the Modern World*, no. 1, translated in Walter M. Abbott (ed.), *The Documents of Vatican II* (New York: Association Press, 1966), pp. 199–200.

CHAPTER 2

1. Letter to the author, dated August 24, 1971.

2. Ernst Bloch, *Das Prinzip Hoffnung* (Frankfurt am Main: Suhrkamp, 1959), p. 1381.

3. Reports 69 and 70 from the Social Institute of the See of Essen: *Religiosität und Kirchlichkeit der Katholiken Bochums* (mimeographed; Essen, 1970 and 1971).

4. Hjalmar Sundén, in his *Die Religion und die Rollen* (Berlin: Töpelmann, 1966), pp. 406–408, tells of a 1948 Gallup poll on survival after death, that was conducted in eleven countries. The results of a further Gallup poll on the same subject, conducted in ten countries in 1968, are given in: "Foi, religion, morale et vie familiale dans dix pays d'Europe," *Social Compass* 18 (1971) 278–284.

5. Cf. Friedrich Heer, *Abschied von Höllen und Himmeln* (Munich: Bechtle, 1970).

6. Sigmund Freud, *The Future of an Illusion*, translated by W. D. Robson-Scott, revised and newly edited by James Strachey (New York: Doubleday, 1964), p. 71.

7. Ibid., pp. 44–45.

8. Gen. 1:28.

9. Elias Canetti, *Crowds and Power*, translated by Carol Stewart (London: Gollancz, 1962), p. 465.

10. John Kenneth Galbraith, *The Affluent Society* (Boston: Houghton Mifflin, 1958), p. 21.

11. Paul A. Baran and Paul M. Sweezy, *Monopoly Capital: An Essay on the American Economic and Social Order* (New York: Monthly Review Press, 1966), p. 109.

12. Robert Musil, *The Man Without Qualities*, translated by Eithne

Wilkins and Ernst Kaiser (New York: Coward, McCann, 1954), 1:360 (in the Capricorn Books reprint of volume 1, 1965).

13. *Macbeth*, act 5, scene 5.

14. Max Horkheimer, *Anfänge der bürgerlichen Geschichtsphilosophie* (Frankfurt am Main: Fischer Bücherei 6014, 1971), p. 68.

15. *Macbeth*, act 5, scene 5.

16. *Hamlet*, act 5, scene 2.

17. G. W. F. Hegel, *Vorlesungen über die Philosophie der Weltgeschichte* (ed. G. Lasson; Leipzig, 1920), p. 12.

18. In *Die Zeit*, November 12, 1971.

19. Talcott Parsons, *The Social System* (London: Routledge and Kegan Paul, 1964), p. 372.

20. Ibid.

21. Michelin, *Italy* (German edition, 1965), p. 163.

22. Bloch, op. cit., p. 227.

23. Opening words for each Hour of the Roman Breviary.

24. 1 John 3:2.

25. From the Roman Mass for the Dead.

26. Karl Jaspers, *Philosophical Faith and Revelation*, translated by E. B. Ashton (New York: Harper & Row, 1967), p. 40.

27. *Sermo* 358, 2 (*PL* 39:1588). Cf. Ps. 118 (119): 96. For more information on Augustine's struggle with the Donatists, cf. F. van der Meer, *Augustine the Bishop: The Life and Work of a Father of the Church*, translated by Brian Battershaw and G. R. Lamb (New York: Sheed & Ward, 1961), chapter 4: "The *Pars Donati* and the Heretics" (pp. 79–128).

28. Cf. Jaspers, op. cit., pp. 41–49; Canetti, op. cit., pp. 154–158.

CHAPTER 3

1. E. O. James, *Prehistoric Religion: A Study in Prehistoric Archaeology* (New York: Barnes and Noble, 1957), pp. 17–20. The following three paragraphs are a summary of these pages, using chiefly James's own language.

2. Ibid., pp. 21–28.

3. Matt. 8:22.

4. Arnold J. Toynbee, *A Study of History*, abridgment of volumes 1–6

by D. C. Somervell (New York: Oxford University Press, 1946), pp. 68–73.

5. Michelin, *Italy* (German edition), p. 102.

6. Jacob Burckhardt, *The Civilization of the Renaissance in Italy*, translated by S. G. C. Middlemore (New York: Harper Torchbooks, 1958), 1:227–228.

7. Sigmund Freud, *Totem and Taboo: Resemblances between the Psychic Lives of Savages and Neurotics*, translated by A. A. Brill (1918; New York: Random House, n.d.), pp. 81–82.

8. Ibid., p. 78.

9. Canetti, op. cit., p. 227.

10. Freud, op. cit., p. 183.

11. Ibid., p. 196.

12. Ibid., p. 183, note 78.

13. Ibid., pp. 182–183.

14. Ibid., p. 207.

CHAPTER 4

1. *Der Spiegel*, no. 53, 1971.

2. Cf. Guy E. Swanson, *The Birth of the Gods: The Origin of Primitive Beliefs* (Ann Arbor: University of Michigan Press, 1960), pp. 32–33.

3. Sir George Grey, *Polynesian Mythology and Ancient Traditional History of the New Zealand Race as Furnished by Their Priests and Chiefs* (London: John Murray, 1855), p. vii.

4. Max Weber, *The Protestant Ethic and the Spirit of Capitalism*, translated by Talcott Parsons (New York: Scribner's, 1958), p. 181. Weber is quoting Richard Baxter, *The Saints' Everlasting Rest* (1650), chapter 12. Cf. Merleau-Ponty, op. cit., pp. 23–24.

5. Paul Parin, Fritz Morgentaler, and Goldy Parin-Mattèy, *Fürchte deinen Nächsten wie dich selbst* (Frankfurt am Main: Suhrkamp, 1971), pp. 188–189.

6. Ibid., p. 186.

7. For the material on the Agni in this and the following five paragraphs, cf. Parin et al., op. cit., pp. 66–69, 108–115, 178–190.

8. Ibid., p. 185.

9. Ibid., p. 549.

10. Cf. *Time*, October 18, 1971, pp. 58–60.

11. *Die Presse*, October 9–10, 1971.

12. I am inclined to think that any traditions the primitives have about a hell derive from missionaries representing the high religions. In this connection I wish to thank Peter Weidkuhn of the Ethnological Seminar at the University of Basel; his valuable suggestions considerably advanced my own thinking. Guy Swanson's excellent book has already been cited.

13. Dominic M. Prümmer, O.P., *Handbook of Moral Theology*, translated from the 1949 edition by Gerald W. Shelton (New York: Kenedy, 1957), p. 379.

14. Ibid., p. 378.

15. Sigmund Freud, "Thoughts for the Times on War and Death," in *Collected Papers*, authorized translation under the supervision of Joan Riviere (New York: Basic Books, 1959), 4:301.

16. The material in this and the next five paragraphs is taken from Robin Fox, *Kinship and Marriage: An Anthropological Perspective* (Baltimore: Penguin, 1967) and is a summary paraphrase of pp. 86–88.

17. Sigmund Freud, *The Future of an Illusion*, pp. 48–49.

18. Ibid., pp. 52–53.

CHAPTER 5

1. Johannes Leipoldt, *Von Epidauros zu Lourdes* (Hamburg-Bergstedt: Herbert Reich Verlag, 1957), p. 9.

2. From Kurt Schmid (ed.), *Buddhas Reden* (Hamburg: Rowohlt, 1961), p. 232.

3. Ibid., pp. 203–205 (abridged).

4. Ludwig Wittgenstein, *Lectures and Conversations on Aesthetics, Psychology and Religious Belief*, edited by Cyril Barrett (Berkeley-Los Angeles: University of California Press, 1966), p. 55.

5. Ibid., p. 53.

6. Cf. Toynbee, op. cit. pp. 12–34.

7. Ibid.

8. Ibid., pp. 375–392.

9. *The Koran*, translated by N. J. Dawood (revised edition; Baltimore: Penguin, 1959), p. 29.

10. *The Koran*, sura 75, p. 54.
11. Toynbee, op. cit., p. 19.
12. Isa. 26:14.
13. Ezek. 37:1–12.
14. Dan. 7:9–10.
15. Dan. 12:2.
16. Rev. 20:13–15.
17. Freud, *The Future of an Illusion*, pp. 77–78.
18. Bertolt Brecht, *Der Jasager und der Neinsager* (Frankfurt am Main: Suhrkamp, 1967), p. 19.
19. Max Weber, *The Religion of India: The Sociology of Hinduism and Buddhism*, translated by Hans H. Gerth and Don Martindale (Glencoe, Ill.: Free Press, 1958), p. 332.
20. Max Weber, "Religious Rejections of the World and Their Directions," in *From Max Weber: Essays in Sociology*, translated by Hans H. Gerth and C. Wright Mills (New York: Oxford University Press, 1946), p. 356.
21. Ibid., pp. 356–357.

CHAPTER 6

1. Elias Canetti, *Die Befristeten* (Munich: Hanswer, 1964).
2. Herbert Nette, *Adieu les belles choses* (Düsseldorf: Eugen Diederichs, 1971).
3. *Sein und Zeit* (1927), translated as *Being and Time* by John Macquarrie and Edward Robinson (New York: Harper & Row, 1962).
4. Evelina Krieger, *Abgrund und Gründe* (Graz: Styria, 1966), p. 180.
5. The letters quoted here were written between April 1964 and October 1966.
6. Krieger, op. cit., p. 176.
7. Bernard Berelson and Gary A. Steiner, *Human Behavior: An Inventory of Scientific Findings* (New York: Harcourt, Brace and World, 1964), chapter 14: "Opinions, Attitudes, and Beliefs."
8. Charles Morris, *Varieties of Human Value* (Chicago: University of Chicago Press, 1956).
9. Cf. Robert Freed Bales, *Personality and Interpersonal Behavior* (New

York: Holt Rinehart and Winston, 1970), pp. 497–501, for the four basic dimensions; the "typical statements" quoted in the next paragraph are from these pages.

10. The three types indicated in this and the next two paragraphs, along with their statements, are from Bales, op. cit., pp. 305–307, 275, and 224 respectively.

11. The types we choose here are listed in Bales as U, P, F, N, B, and D.

12. Musil, op. cit., 2:191.

13. Ibid., p. 193.

14. Ibid.

15. Ibid., p. 198.

16. Walter Hinz, *Geborgenheit* (Zürich: Arthur Brunner, 1971).

17. Ibid., 45–48.

18. This and the following data and quotations are from Hinz, op. cit., pp. 32–36 (with bibliography).

19. Augustine, *De praedestinatione sanctorum*, 2, 5: "Nullus quippe credit aliquid, nisi prius cogitaverit esse credendum."

20. In my edition of the *Clavis Coeli* by Martin von Cochem (died 1712), the title page is missing; pagination begins only after the "Explanation of the Fearful Torments of Purgatory" (54 pages long), at the start of the "Prayerbook" (600 pages). Martin von Cochem composed about thirty prayerbooks. A complete bibliography of his works is now being prepared.

21. Cf. Herbert Haag, *Abschied vom Teufel* (Einsiedeln: Benziger, 1969).

22. Any of the better bookstores will acquaint you with the current popular and scientific books on parapsychology.

CHAPTER 7

1. *Die Presse*, April 18, 1972.

2. Theodor W. Adorno, *Minima Moralia: Reflections from a Damaged Life*, translated by E. F. N. Jephcott (London: NLB, 1974), p. 247.

3. 2 Macc. 1:19–22.

4. Dated January 4, 1972.

5. Adorno, op. cit., p. 247.

6. Luke 23:43.

7. Ludwig Ott, *Grundriss der katholischen Dogmatik* (Freiburg: Herder,

1952), pp. 541–566. The English translation is by J. Patrick Lynch (St. Louis: B. Herder, 1954); cf. pp. 474–494. The chapter- and section-titles, as well as the propositions of faith, are cited from the English translation. The passage on the Scriptural proof of hell is from p. 478.

8. Pascal, *Pensées*, Lafuma no. 340, Brunschvicg no. 218; translated by Martin Turnell, *Pascal's Pensées* (New York: Harper, 1962), p. 200.

9. *Pensées*, Laf. no. 343, Br. no. 233; translated by Turnell, op. cit., pp. 201–204.

10. Jean Paul [Johann Paul Friedrich Richter], *Blumen-, Frucht- und Dornenstücke oder Ehestand, Tod und Hochzeit des Armenadvokaten F. St. Siebenkäs* (1796–1797).

11. Freud, *The Future of an Illusion*, p. 81.

12. Adorno, op. cit., p. 61.

CHAPTER 8

1. *Kronen-Zeitung*, October 26, 1971.

2. We may add that on July 2, 1972, Marko had a serious accident at Clermont-Ferrand and injured his left eye. Helmut Marko, with a doctorate in law, said in an interview in December 1972: "There was the pain and all the thoughts! Night after night I couldn't sleep. I thought of a hundred possibilities, rejected them, and went back over them again. Then I realized that the only real possibility was the hundred and first: to get out of racing!" (*Die Presse*, December 23, 1972).

3. *Hamlet*, act 1, scene 5.

4. Döblin, op. cit., p. 635.

5. Cf. F. A. Whitlock, *Death on the Road* (London: Tavistock, 1971).

6. Rom. 5:12.

7. Cf. Edward Goldsmith and Robert Allen, *Planspiel zum Überleben* (Stuttgart: Deutsche Verlags-Anstalt, 1972), especially pp. 60–80.

8. The reference is to the Book of Lamentations. In the Roman liturgy the Lamentations are sung in the Tenebrae Service on Holy Thursday, Good Friday, and Holy Saturday. The polyphonic singing in the service at Vienna (Cathedral of St. Stephen) is regarded as artistically superb.

9. This consumer advocate became famous through his book *Unsafe at Any Speed* (New York: Grossmann, 1965).

10. *Time*, January 17, 1972.
11. Cf. Parin et al., op. cit., pp. 557–559.
12. Mark 14:32–37.

CHAPTER 9

1. Simone de Beauvoir, *The Coming of Age*, translated by Patrick O'Brian (New York: Putnam, 1972). These three paragraphs are a paraphrase of pp. 238–239.
2. Letters of August 2, 1971, and January 4, 1972.
3. de Beauvoir, op. cit., p. 2.
4. Ibid., p. 5.
5. Harold L. Sheppard, *Toward an Industrial Gerontology* (Cambridge, Mass.: Schenkmann, 1970).
6. The story is titled "Die Lebenszeit" ("The Lifespan"). A full translation of it may be found in *The Frog King and Other Tales of the Brothers Grimm*, translated by Alfred and Mary Elizabeth David (New York: New American Library, 1964), pp. 285–287.
7. The passage is from the third section of the biblical Book of Isaiah, or Trito-Isaiah, and can be dated with some assurance between 538 and 515 B.C. The important thing about it is that the poor are collectively regarded as elect; this is something new in the history of religions.
8. Cf. the letter of January 4, 1972, quoted in chapter 7.
9. Mark 14:66–72.

CHAPTER 10

1. Augustine, *Confessions* I, 4, 4.
2. Barney G. Glaser and Anselm L. Strauss, *Awareness of Dying* (Chicago: Aldine, 1965), pp. 29, 47, 64, 79.
3. Documentation in Glaser and Strauss, op. cit., p. 119.
4. Ibid., pp. 68–69.
5. Ibid., p. 22.
6. Ibid., p. 31.
7. Mark 15:33–37.

CHAPTER 11

1. Cf. Erwin Stengel, *Selbstmord und Selbstmordversuch* (Frankfurt am Main: Fischer, 1969), p. 109; the figures are for Great Britain and include unsuccessful attempts at suicide. In the United States about twelve hundred books on suicide were published between 1957 and 1972; cf. *Time*, June 12, 1972.

2. This and the next quotation are from *City of God* I, 17.

3. Isa. 66:24.

4. Matt. 5:30.

5. J. W. Goethe, *Werke* (ed. Mathiesen, 1949), 4:299.

6. Canetti, *Crowds and Power*, p. 66.

7. The story is told in Jacob Burckhardt, *Griechische Kulturgeschichte* 2 (edition of 1956), p. 385.

8. The story and the quotations are from Reinhold Schneider, *Philipp der Zweite, oder Religion und Macht* (Frankfurt am Main: Fischer Bücherei, 1953), pp. 5–6.

9. "The Theme of the Three Caskets" (1903) in *Collected Papers*, 4:256. Freud's illness began in 1923 and necessitated twenty-three operations on his jaw; cf. Max Schnur, *Freud Living and Dying* (New York: International Universities Press, 1972).

10. On the death instinct, cf. Igor A. Caruso, *Die Trennung der Liebenden* (Bern: Hans Huber, 1968).

11. Freud, *The Ego and the Id*, translated by James Strachey (New York: Norton, 1960), p. 57.

12. Job 3:1–2, 13, 16.

13. Cf. his essay, "Religious Rejections of the World and Their Directions," in *From Max Weber: Essays in Sociology*, pp. 323–359.

14. Mark 15:42–46.

CHAPTER 12

1. Matt. 10:8.

2. Merleau-Ponty, op. cit., p. 16.

3. The first literary traces of (unsuccessful) protest are to be found in Egypt, ca. 2000 B.C. The period when the biblical eschatology was formed

(last day, general judgment, heaven, and hell) I would place between 500 B.C. and A.D. 500. A.D. 500 to A.D. 1500 was a period when the biblical eschatology was universally accepted in the Christian West.

4. John 9:4.

5. Rev. 8:13.

6. Dennis L. Meadows et al., *The Limits to Growth: A Report for the Club of Rome's Project on the Predicament of Mankind* (Washington, D.C.: Potomac Association, 1972), pp. 188–189. Pp. 185 ff. contain the Executive Committee's commentary on the report.

7. Ibid., p. 195.

8. Ibid., pp. 192–193.

9. In Oskar Schatz (ed.), *Hat die Religion Zukunft?* (Graz: Styria, 1971), pp. 120–134.

10. Matt. 18:3.

11. In the last five years there have been about five thousand publications, in English alone, on the problem of aggression.

12. Theodor W. Adorno, et al., *The Authoritarian Personality* (New York: Harper & Row, 1950).

13. Milton Rokeach, *The Open and Closed Mind* (New York: Basic Books, 1960).

14. Max Horkheimer and Theodor W. Adorno, *Dialectic of Enlightenment*, translated by John Cumming (New York: Herder and Herder, 1972), p. ix.

15. Bales, op. cit., p. 165.

16. Ibid., p. 221. The discussion being summarized here is on pp. 220–228.

17. Musil, op. cit., 2:198.

CHAPTER 13

1. *Die Presse*, July 1–2, 1972.

2. G. F. Handel, *Der Messias*, edited by Heinrich Kralik (Vienna: Steyrermühl, n.d.), p. 3.

3. Kralik, op. cit., pp. 12–13.

4. Sigmund Freud, *Civilization and Its Discontents*, translated by James Strachey (New York: Norton, 1961), p. 92.

5. Ibid., p. 69.

6. Mark 10:17–21.

7. Mark 10:22.

8. Max Horkheimer, *Die Sehnsucht nach dem ganz Anderen* (Hamburg: Furche, 1970), p. 77.

9. Peter Handke, *Short Letter, Long Farewell*, translated by Ralph Mannheim (New York: Farrar, Straus and Giroux, 1974), pp. 140–141.

10. Hans Kessler, *Die theologische Bedeutung des Todes Jesu* (Düsseldorf: Patmos, 1970).

11. Ibid., p. 235.

12. Ibid., pp. 241, 252, 294–296, 325–329.

13. Ibid., pp. 83–165.

14. Freud, *Civilization and Its Discontents*, p. 88. Cf. R. S. Lee, *Freud and Christianity* (Harmondsworth: Penguin, 1967), especially pp. 146–152, where the structure of superego religion is discussed. (In my earlier book, *Jesus in Bad Company* [translated by Simon King; New York: Holt, Rinehart, and Winston, 1972], I had already called attention to Lee's work, but did not manage to draw the attention of any of my theologian reviewers to it.)

15. Op. cit., pp. 88–89.

16. Cf. Ludwig Wittgenstein, *On Certainty*, edited by G. E. Anscombe and G. H. von Wright, and translated by Denis Paul and G. E. Anscombe (New York: J. and J. Harper, 1969).

CHAPTER 14

1. John 20:19–29.

2. *Kronen-Zeitung*, July 15, 1972.

3. Cf. Samuel N. Kramer, *The Sumerians* (Chicago: University of Chicago Press, 1963), pp. 153–155.

4. Op. cit., pp. 65–66.

5. Correct answer: no.

CHAPTER 15

1. Régine Pernoud, *The Retrial of Joan of Arc: The Evidence at the Trial for Her Rehabilitation, 1450–1456*, translated by J. M. Cohen (New York: Harcourt, Brace, 1955), p. 194.

2. Ibid.

3. Cf. the German translation of the trial record, *Der Prozess Jeanne d'Arc* (Munich: Deutsche Taschenbuch Verlag, 1961), pp. 18–19.

4. The following dialogue consists of exchanges on several occasions; cf. *Der Prozess Jeanne d'Arc*, pp. 20, 28, 68, 30.

5. This last exchange is in Lucien Fabre, *Joan of Arc*, translated by Gerard Hopkins (New York: McGraw–Hill, 1954), p. 274.

6. Ibid., p. 315.

7. *Der Prozess Jeanne d'Arc*, p. 207.

8. Pernoud, op. cit., p. 209.

9. Ibid., pp. 183–184.

10. Ibid., pp. 209–210.

11. Fabre, op. cit., p. 318.

12. Cf. Werner Fuchs, *Todesbilder in der modernen Gesellschaft* (Frankfurt am Main: Suhrkamp, 1969), pp. 101–113.

13. *Der Prozess Jeanne d'Arc*, p. 59.

14. [The German word for "concept," *Begriff*, means literally "an act of grasping or seizing" or "something grasped or seized."]

15. *Der Prozess Jeanne d'Arc*, pp. 203–204.

16. *Der Prozess Jeanne d'Arc*, p. 209.

17. Pernoud, op. cit., pp. 216–217.

CHAPTER 16

1. "Gespräch mit Elias Canetti," *Literatur und Kritik*, no. 65 (June, 1972), p. 274.

2. Ibid.

3. Ibid., p. 277.

4. Quoted in W. G. Sebald, "Gedanken zu Elias Canetti," *Literatur und Kritik*, no. 65 (1972), p. 284.

5. Canetti, *Crowds and Power*, pp. 207–209.

6. Ibid., pp. 155–156.

7. Quoted by Norman Mailer, *Of a Fire on the Moon* (Boston: Little, Brown, 1970), p. 76.

8. Ibid., p. 57.

9. Ibid., p. 58.

10. Ibid., p. 121.